This book belongs to:

....

Mrs Wordsmith®

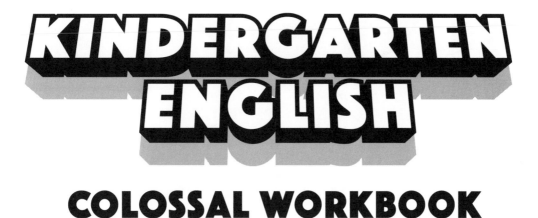

KINDERGARTEN ENGLISH

COLOSSAL WORKBOOK

Bearnice

Bogart

Brick

Plato

Grit

Yin & Yang

Armie

Shang High

Oz

MEET THE
CHARACTERS

CONTENTS

LETTERS & SOUNDS

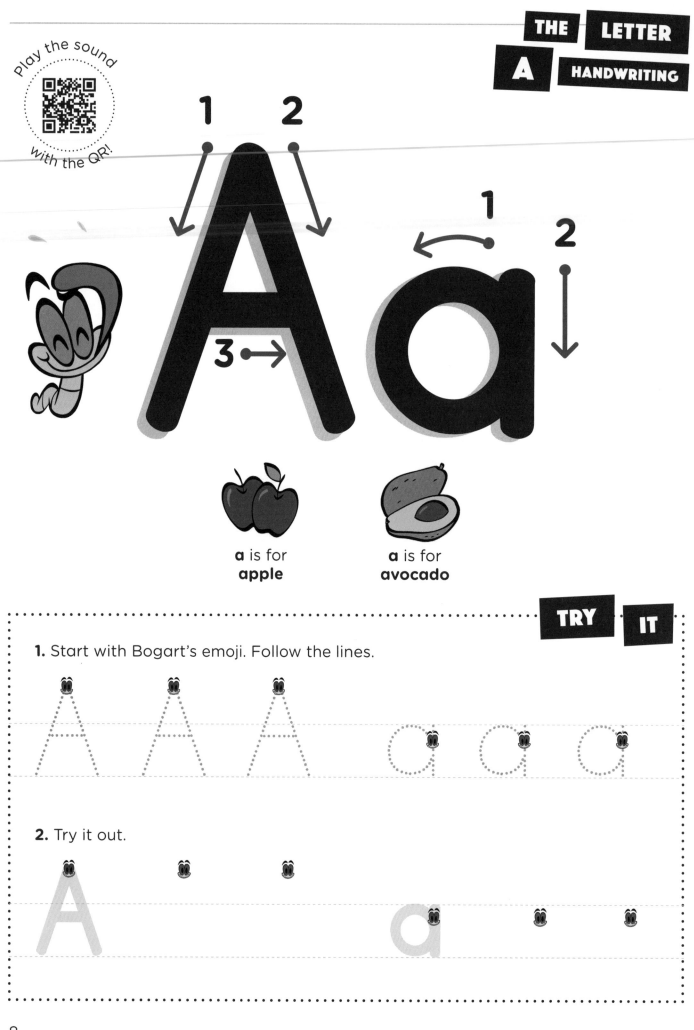

1 2

1 2

3 →

a is for
apple

a is for
avocado

TRY IT

1. Start with Bogart's emoji. Follow the lines.

2. Try it out.

Play the sound with the QR!

1 2 1

2

b is for
banana

b is for
burger

b is for
bread

b is for
blueberries

1. Start with Bogart's emoji. Follow the lines.

B B B b b b

2. Try it out.

B b

c is for
cake

c is for
carrot

c is for
cabbage

c is for
corn

TRY IT

1. Start with Bogart's emoji. Follow the lines.

2. Try it out.

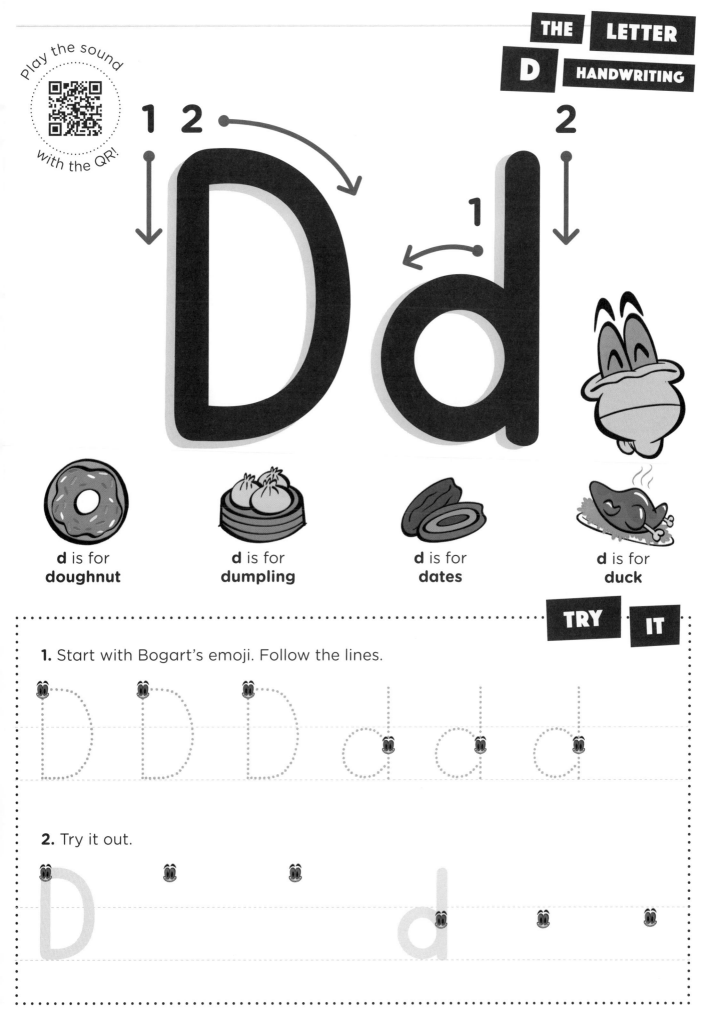

Play the sound with the QR!

1 2

2

1

d is for
doughnut

d is for
dumpling

d is for
dates

d is for
duck

TRY **IT**

1. Start with Bogart's emoji. Follow the lines.

2. Try it out.

Play the sound with the QR!

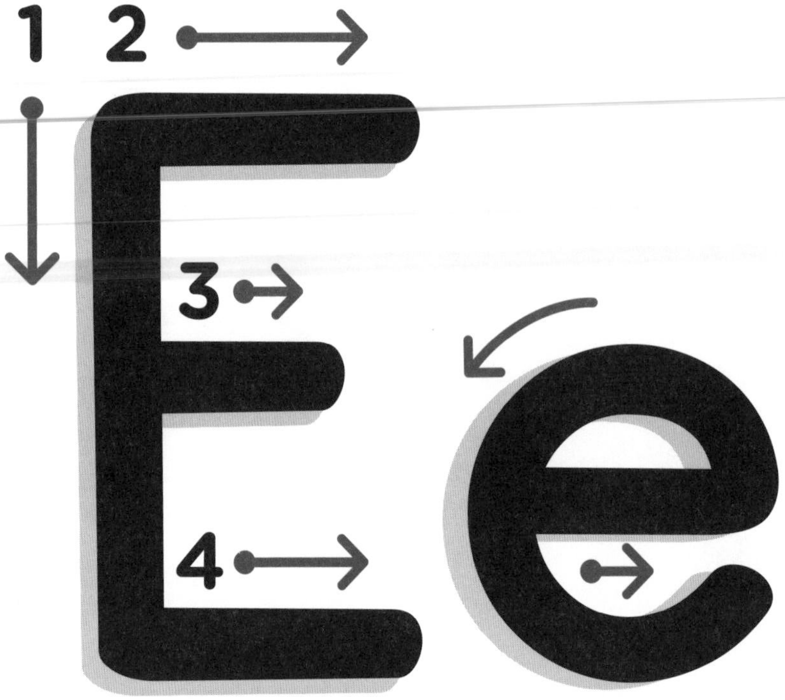

1 2 →

3 →

4 →

e is for
edamame

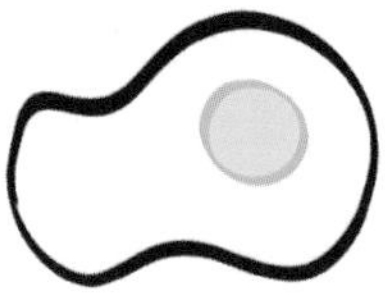

e is for
egg

1. Start with Bogart's emoji. Follow the lines.

E E E E e e e

2. Try it out.

E e

1 2 →
3 →

f
2 →
1

f is for
falafel

f is for
figs

f is for
flour

f is for
fries

TRY IT

1. Start with Bogart's emoji. Follow the lines.

2. Try it out.

Play the sound with the QR!

g is for
granola

g is for
grapefruit

g is for
grapes

g is for
garlic

TRY IT

1. Start with Bogart's emoji. Follow the lines.

2. Try it out.

14

Play the sound with the QR!

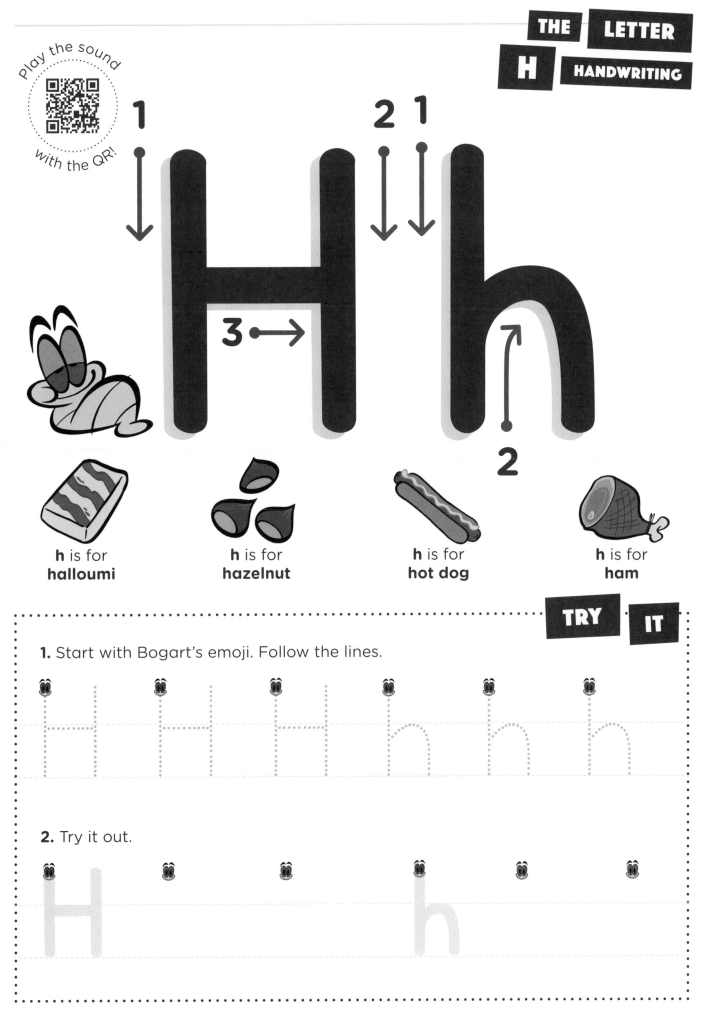

1

2 1

3 →

2

h is for
halloumi

h is for
hazelnut

h is for
hot dog

h is for
ham

TRY IT

1. Start with Bogart's emoji. Follow the lines.

2. Try it out.

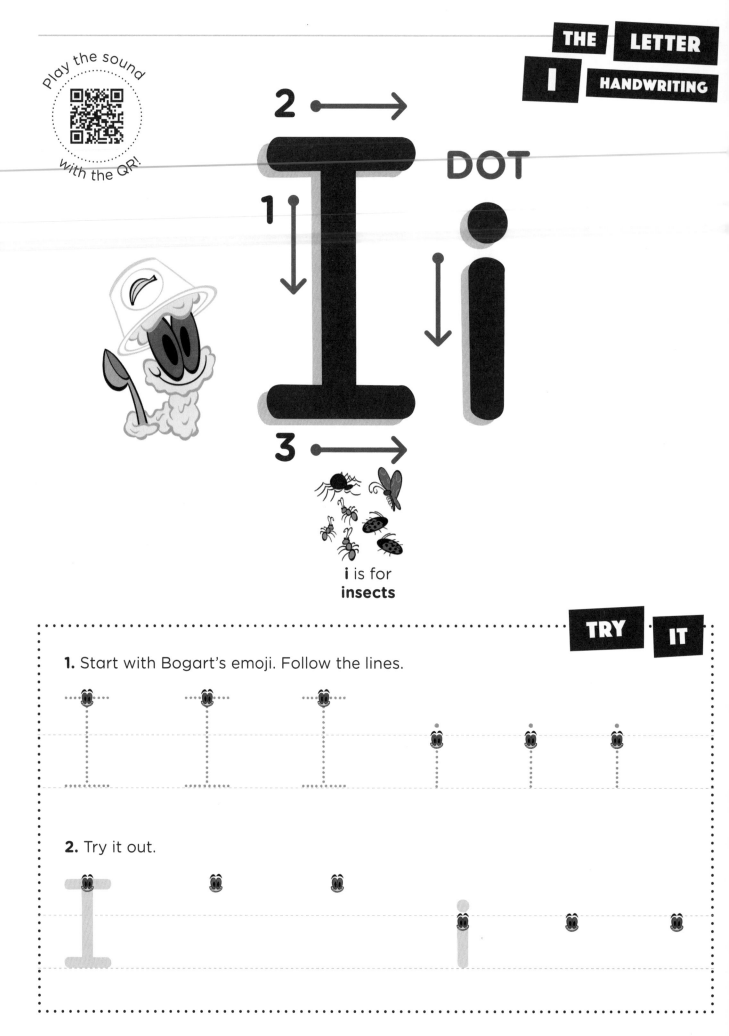

Play the sound with the QR!

2 →

DOT

1 ↓

↓

3 →

i is for
insects

TRY IT

1. Start with Bogart's emoji. Follow the lines.

2. Try it out.

Play the sound with the QR!

2 →

DOT

1

Jj

j is for
jackfruit

j is for
jelly

j is for
jello

j is for
juice

1. Start with Bogart's emoji. Follow the lines.

2. Try it out.

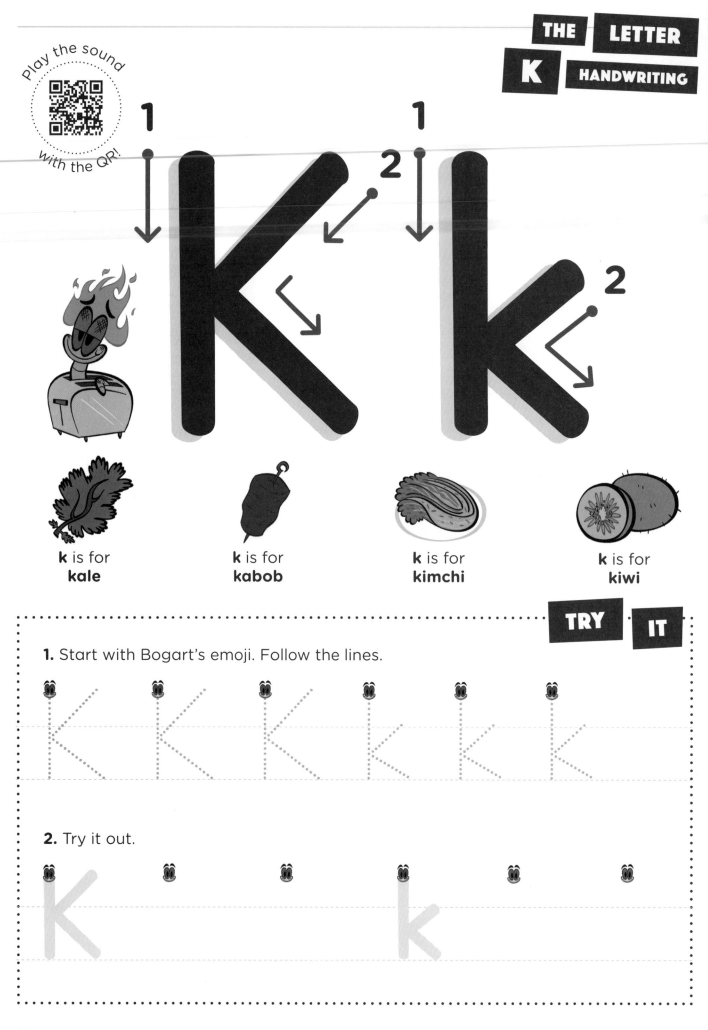

k is for
kale

k is for
kabob

k is for
kimchi

k is for
kiwi

TRY IT

1. Start with Bogart's emoji. Follow the lines.

2. Try it out.

Play the sound with the QR!

Ll

l is for **lemon**

l is for **lentils**

l is for **lettuce**

l is for **lamb**

TRY IT

1. Start with Bogart's emoji. Follow the lines.

2. Try it out.

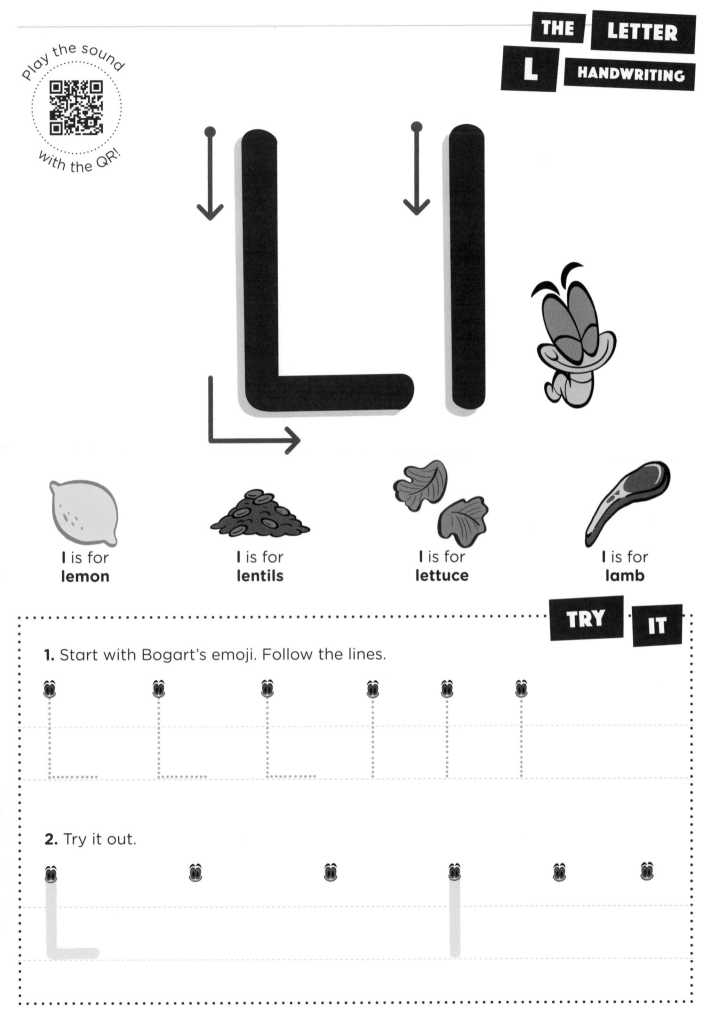

19

Play the sound
with the QR!

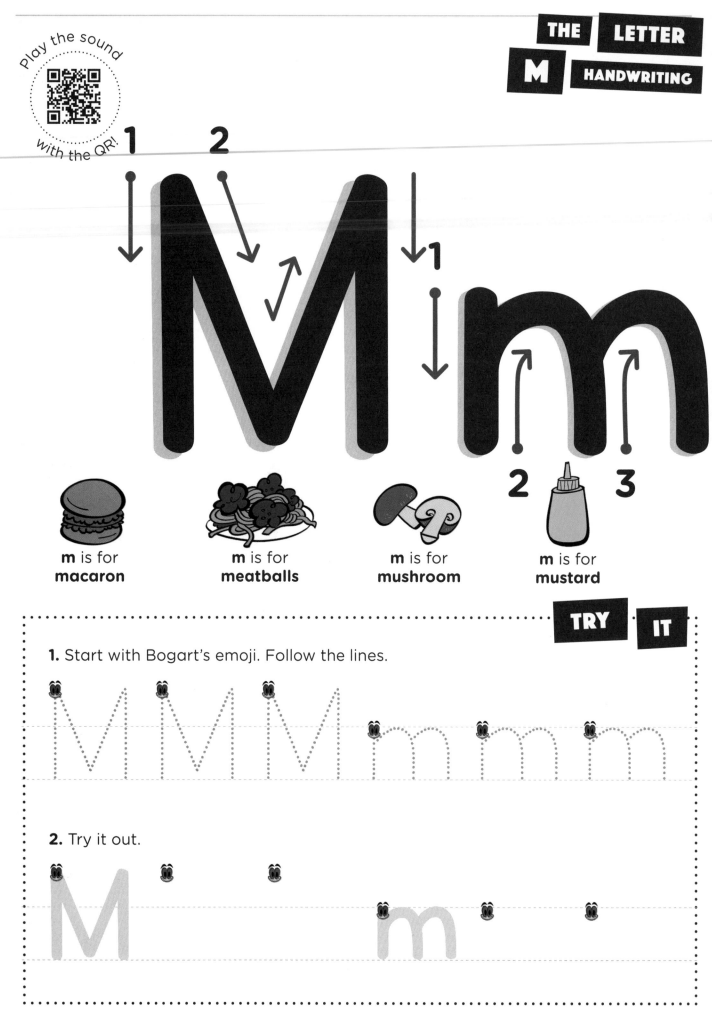

1 2

1

1

2 3

m is for
macaron

m is for
meatballs

m is for
mushroom

m is for
mustard

TRY IT

1. Start with Bogart's emoji. Follow the lines.

M M M m m m

2. Try it out.

M m

20

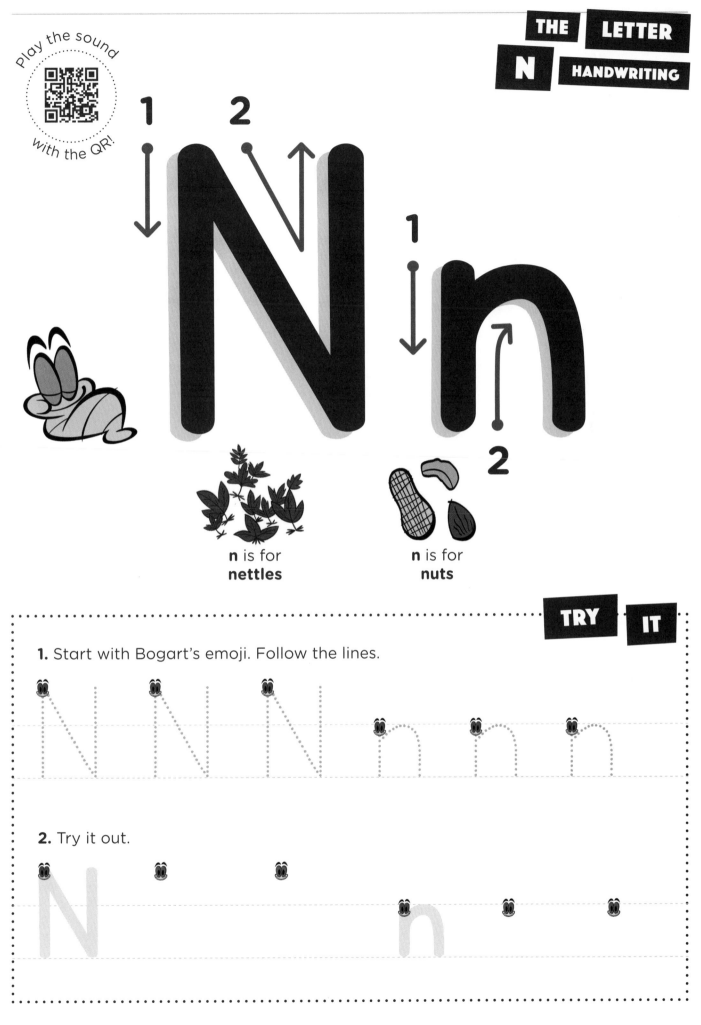

n is for
nettles

n is for
nuts

TRY IT

1. Start with Bogart's emoji. Follow the lines.

2. Try it out.

Play the sound with the QR!

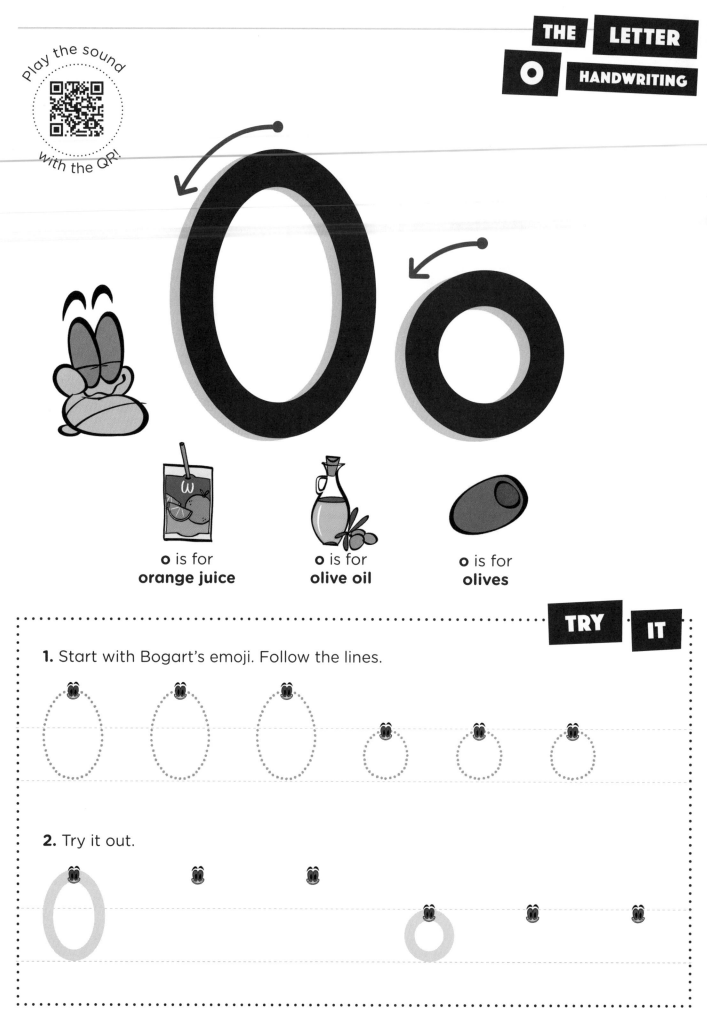

o is for
orange juice

o is for
olive oil

o is for
olives

TRY IT

1. Start with Bogart's emoji. Follow the lines.

2. Try it out.

Play the sound with the QR!

1 2 P

1 2 p

p is for **pancakes**

p is for **passion fruit**

p is for **pepper**

p is for **plum**

TRY IT

1. Start with Bogart's emoji. Follow the lines.

P P P p p p

2. Try it out.

P p

23

Play the sound with the QR!

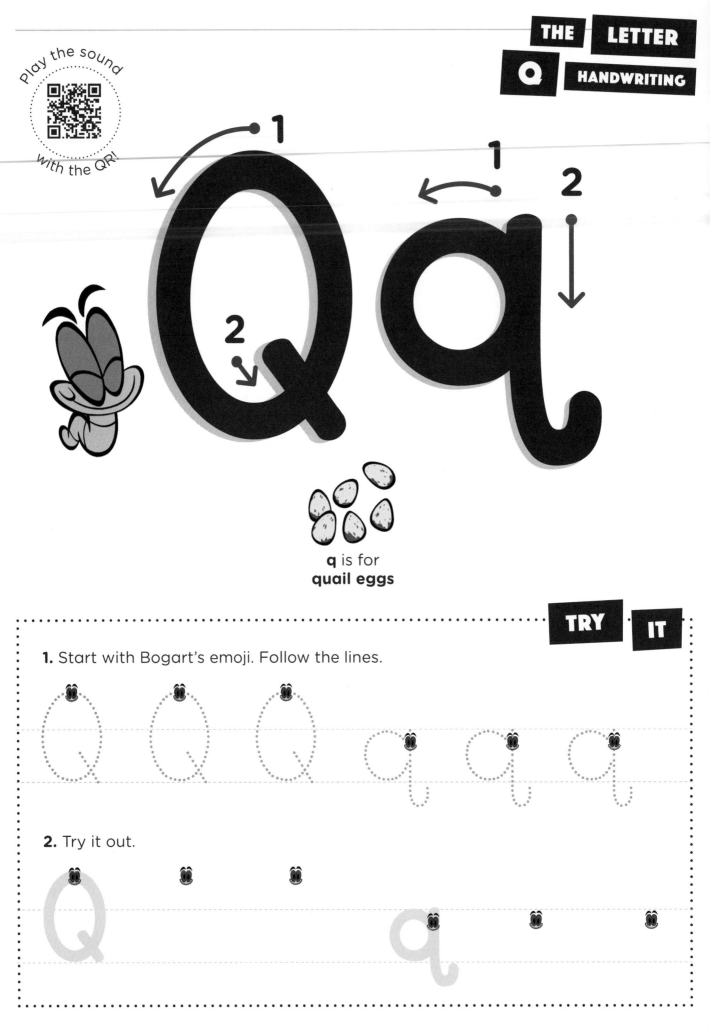

1

2

1

2

q is for
quail eggs

TRY IT

1. Start with Bogart's emoji. Follow the lines.

2. Try it out.

Play the sound with the QR!

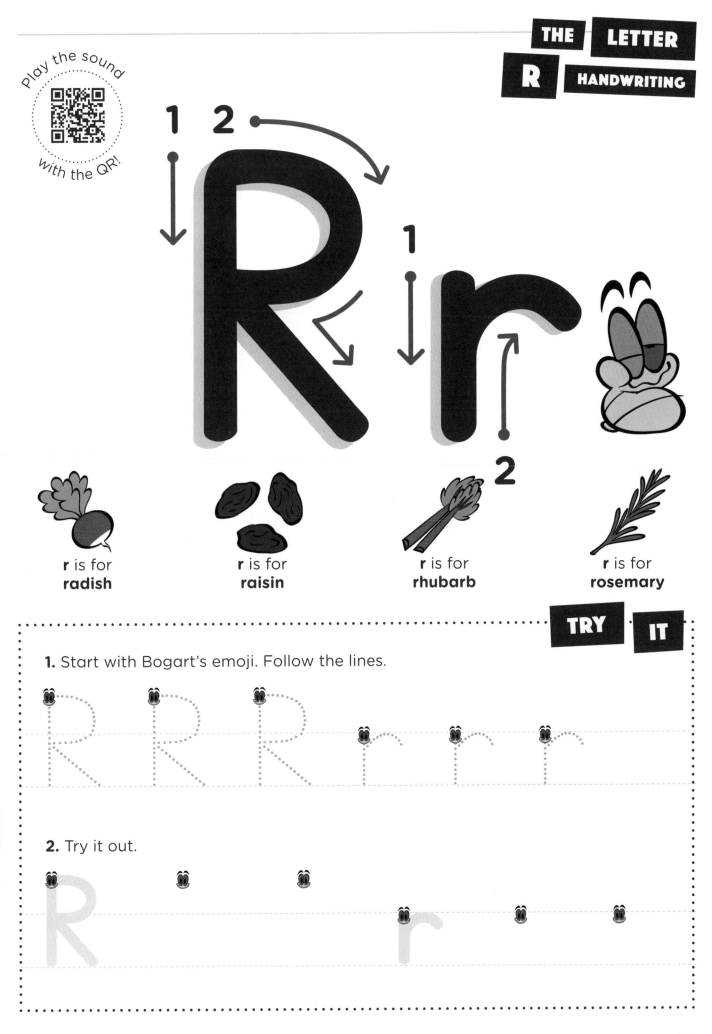

r is for
radish

r is for
raisin

r is for
rhubarb

r is for
rosemary

TRY IT

1. Start with Bogart's emoji. Follow the lines.

RRRrrr

2. Try it out.

R   r

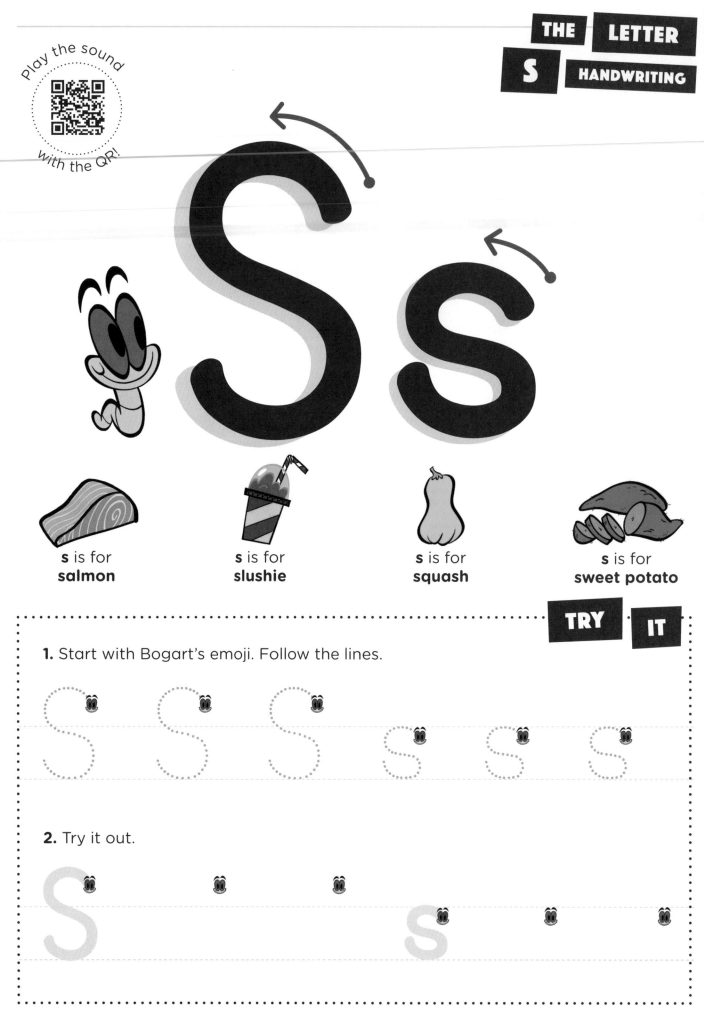

Play the sound with the QR!

s is for
salmon

s is for
slushie

s is for
squash

s is for
sweet potato

TRY IT

1. Start with Bogart's emoji. Follow the lines.

2. Try it out.

26

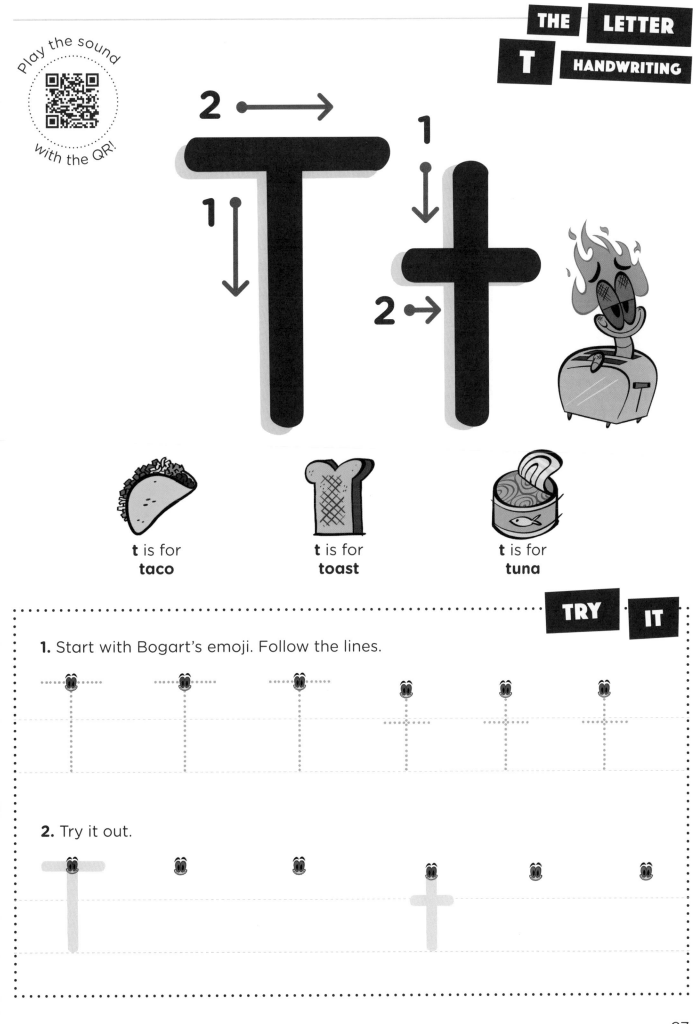

Play the sound with the QR!

2 → →
1 ↓

1 ↓
2 →

t is for
taco

t is for
toast

t is for
tuna

TRY IT

1. Start with Bogart's emoji. Follow the lines.

2. Try it out.

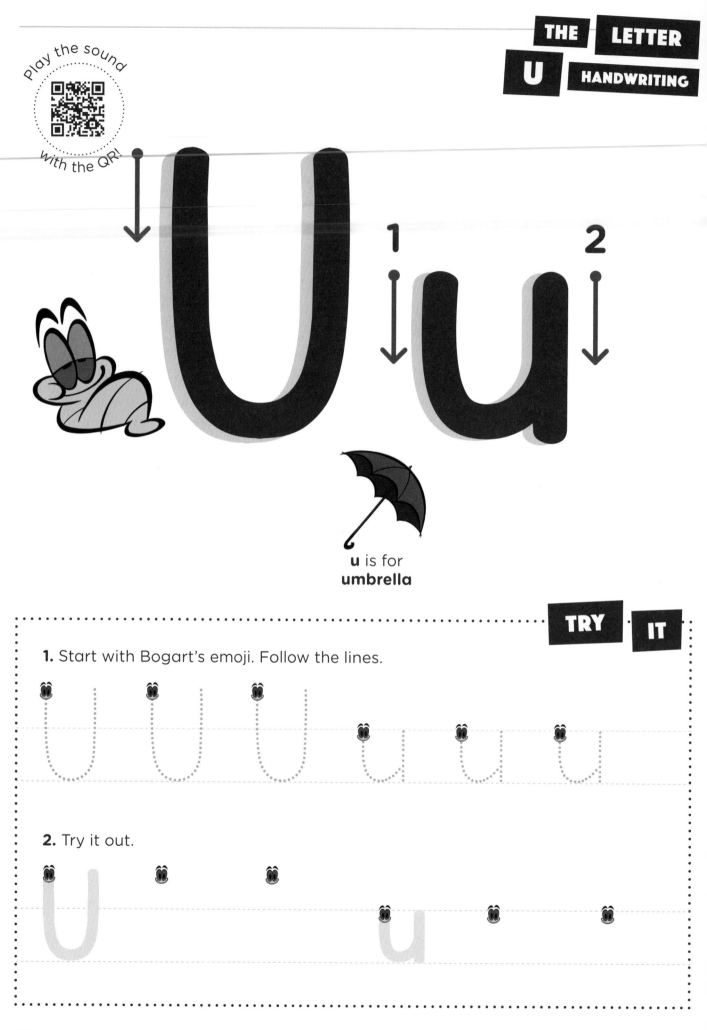

u is for
umbrella

1. Start with Bogart's emoji. Follow the lines.

2. Try it out.

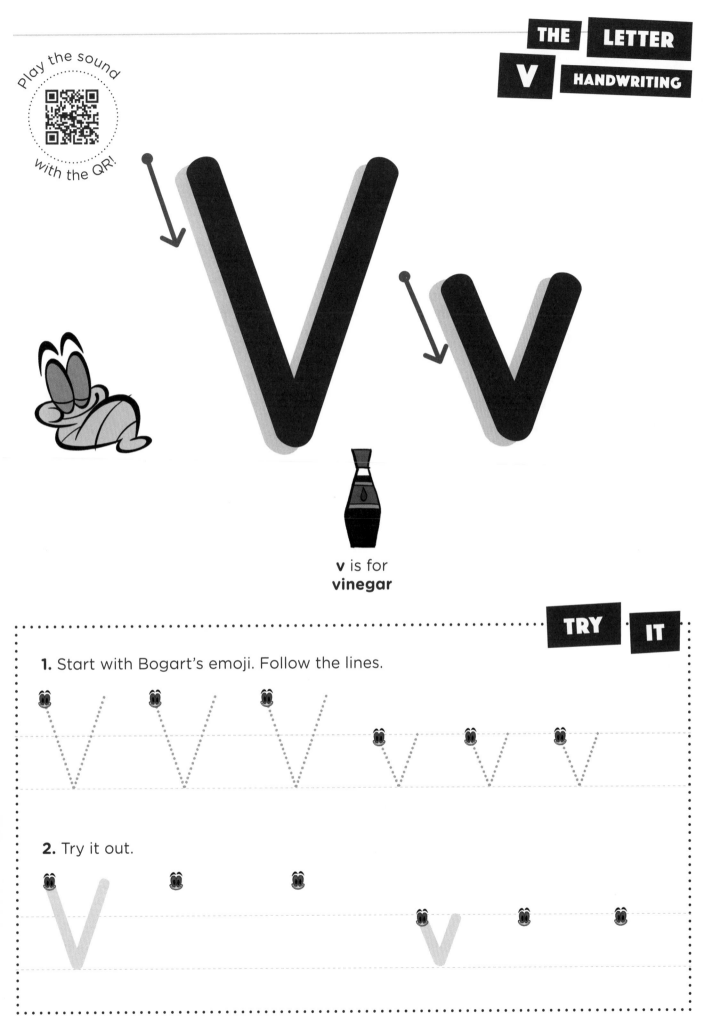

v is for
vinegar

TRY IT

1. Start with Bogart's emoji. Follow the lines.

2. Try it out.

Play the sound with the QR!

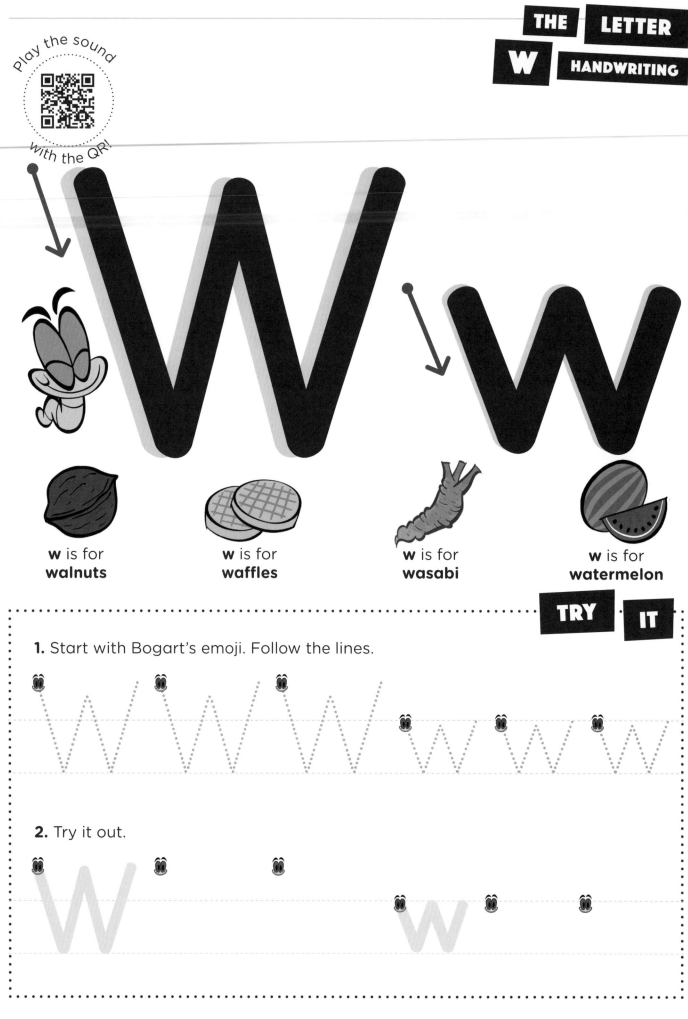

w is for
walnuts

w is for
waffles

w is for
wasabi

w is for
watermelon

TRY IT

1. Start with Bogart's emoji. Follow the lines.

2. Try it out.

Play the sound with the QR!

1   2

1   2

x is for
e**x**tra lu**x**urious
Xmas cookies

TRY IT

1. Start with Bogart's emoji. Follow the lines.

2. Try it out.

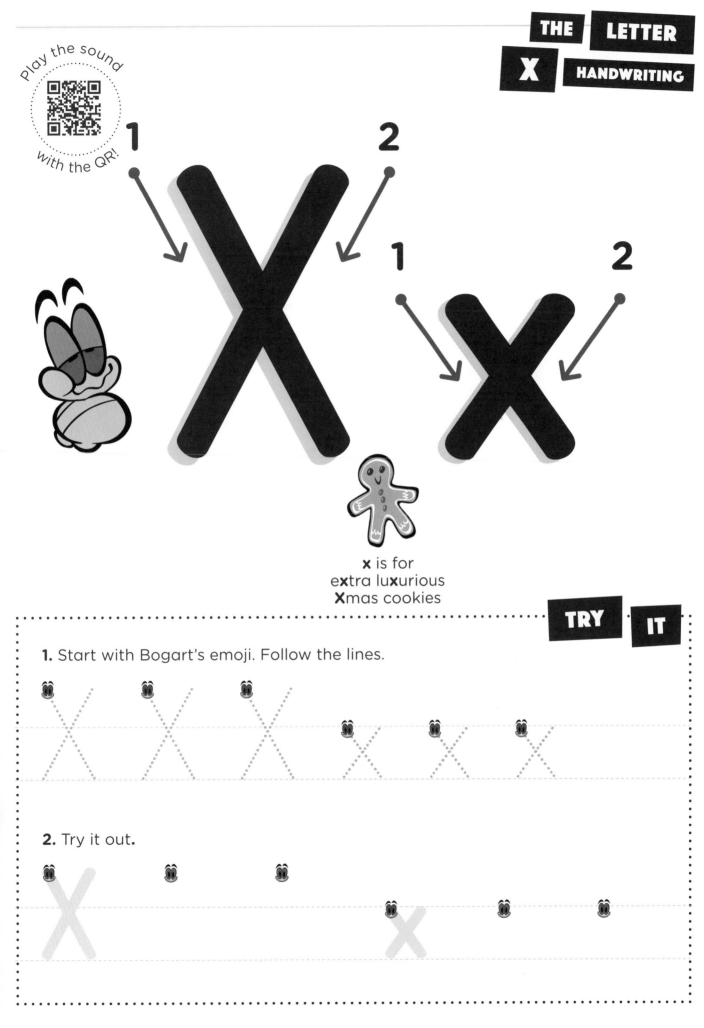

Play the sound with the QR!

1

2

1

2

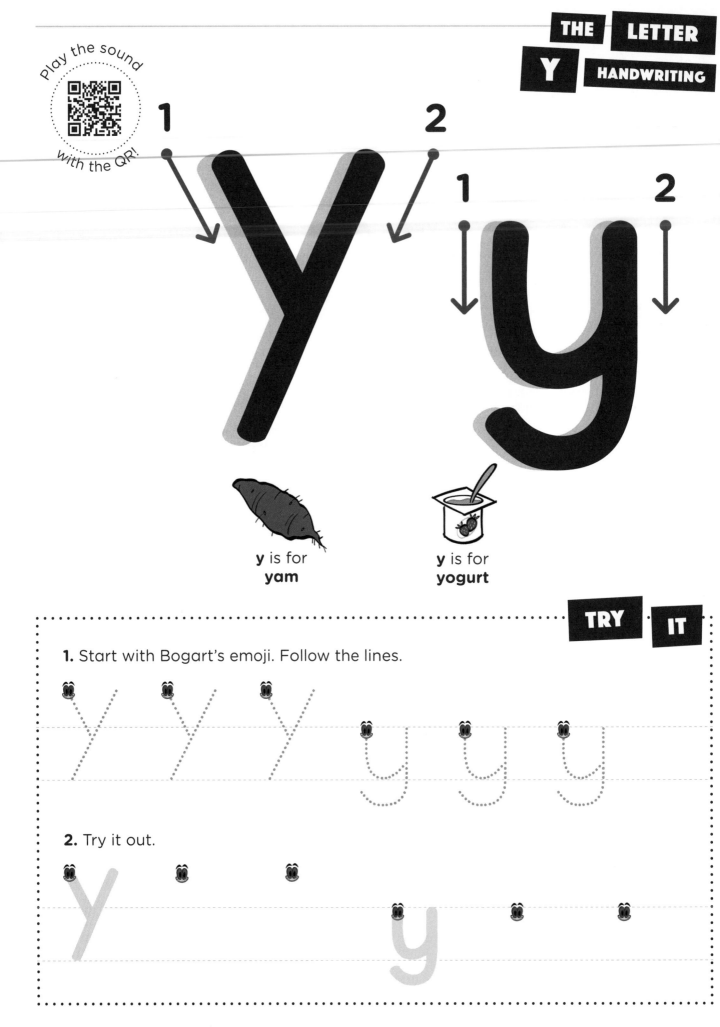

y is for
yam

y is for
yogurt

TRY **IT**

1. Start with Bogart's emoji. Follow the lines.

y y y y y y

2. Try it out.

y y

Play the sound with the QR!

z is for
zebra

1. Start with Bogart's emoji. Follow the lines.

2. Try it out.

33

34

Trace the letters.

A B C D E F G

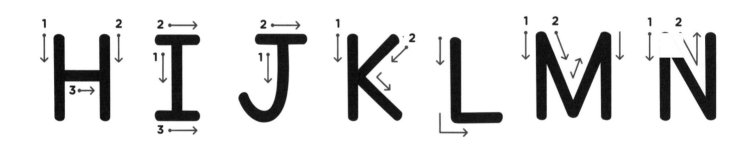

H I J K L M N

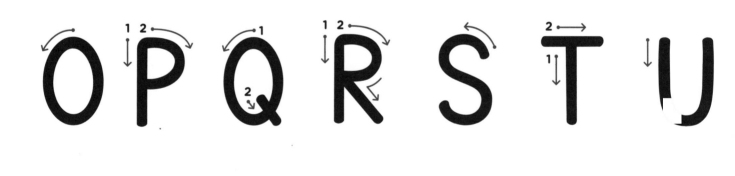

O P Q R S T U

V W X Y Z

Trace the letters.

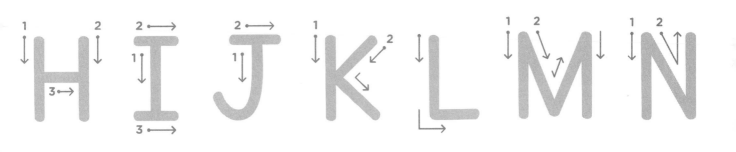

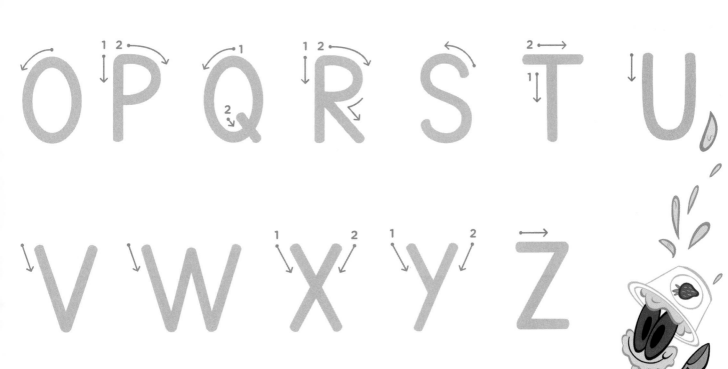

37

Write the alphabet letters in the correct order.

38

Cross out each letter as you place it in order on the opposite page.

G F Q E C K

N Z M T L J

X A R D P I

H S W V U Y

B O

CONFUSING LETTERS:
b and d

Some letters look alike. Be careful when you read them and write them!
Use the word "bed" to remember the difference between b and d.

p and q

Use the words "prince" and "queen" to remember
the difference between p and q.

1. Trace the letter.

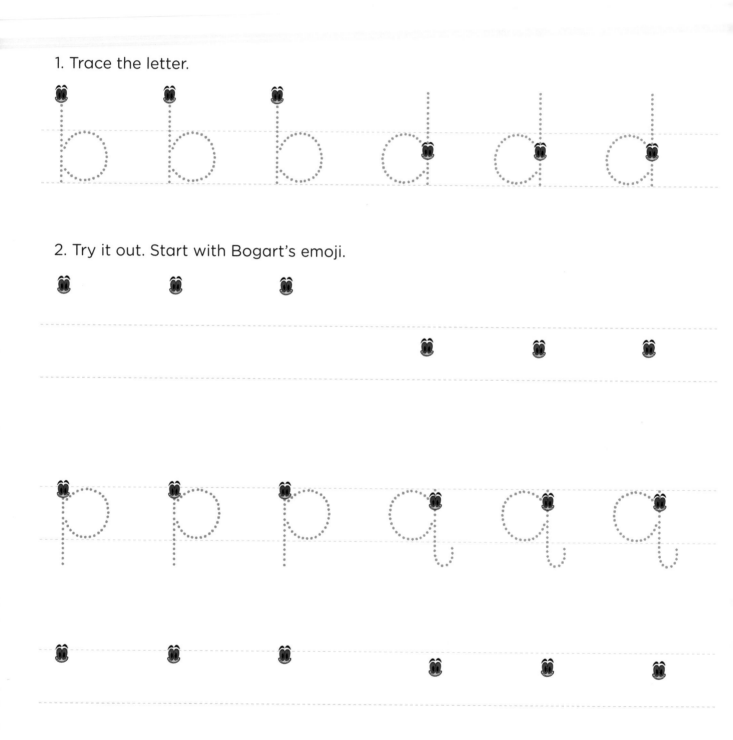

2. Try it out. Start with Bogart's emoji.

Try to spot the differences by coloring the letters like this:

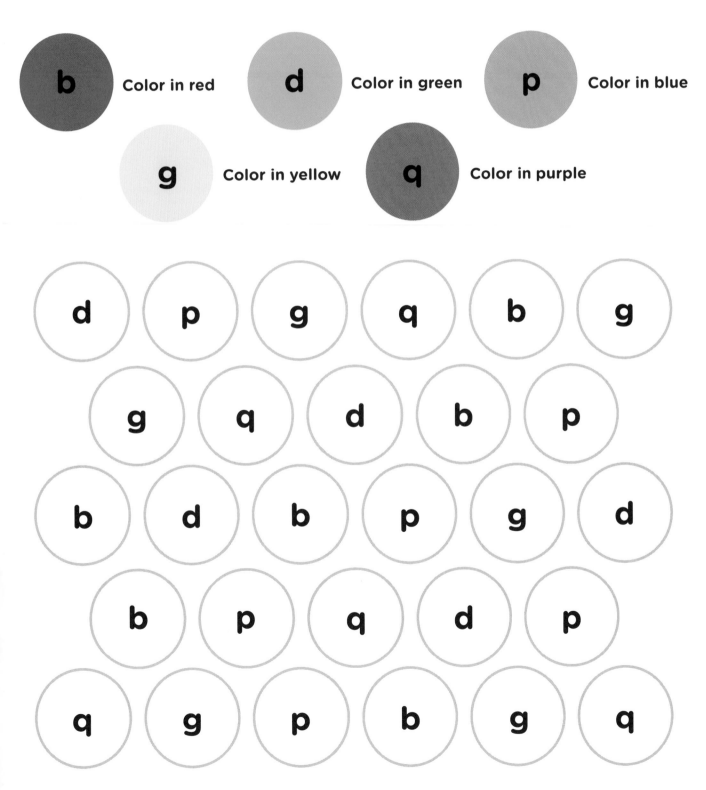

b Color in red

d Color in green

p Color in blue

g Color in yellow

q Color in purple

PHONICS

PHONICS INSTRUCTIONS FOR GROWN-UPS

1

Say to your child, "This is the letter b." Scan the QR code with your mobile phone camera to hear the sound. Tell your child, "This is the sound the letter b makes. Can you copy this sound?" Repeat.

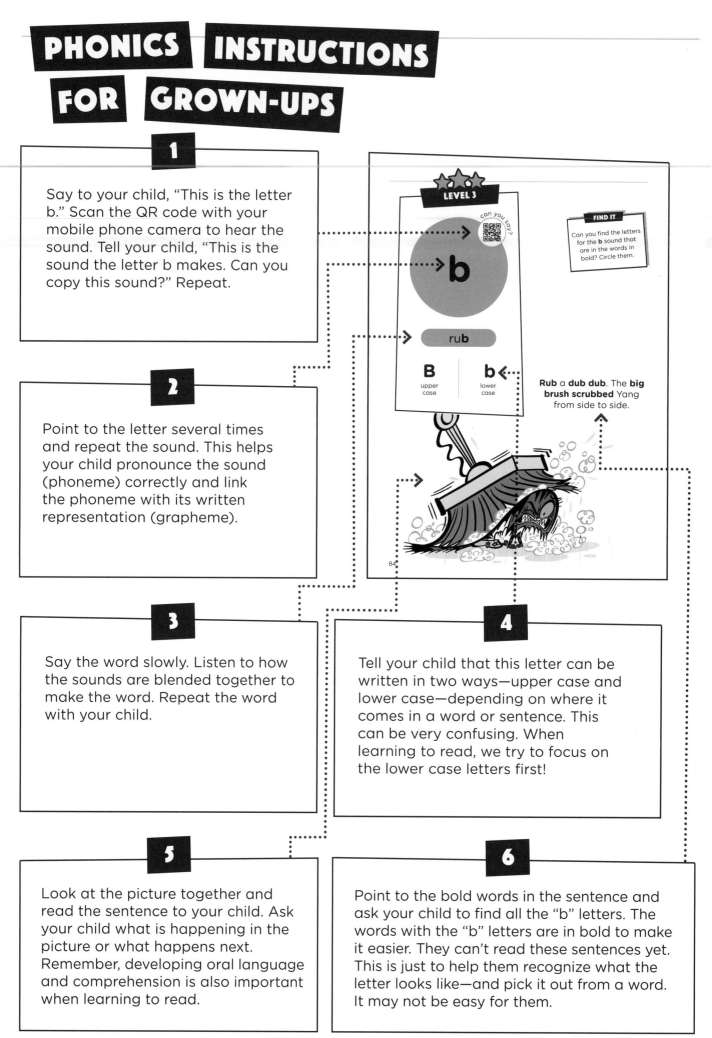

LEVEL 3

can you say?

b

rub

B
upper case

b
lower case

FIND IT

Can you find the letters for the **b** sound that are in the words in bold? Circle them.

Rub a **dub dub**. The **big brush scrubbed** Yang from side to side.

84

2

Point to the letter several times and repeat the sound. This helps your child pronounce the sound (phoneme) correctly and link the phoneme with its written representation (grapheme).

3

Say the word slowly. Listen to how the sounds are blended together to make the word. Repeat the word with your child.

4

Tell your child that this letter can be written in two ways—upper case and lower case—depending on where it comes in a word or sentence. This can be very confusing. When learning to read, we try to focus on the lower case letters first!

5

Look at the picture together and read the sentence to your child. Ask your child what is happening in the picture or what happens next. Remember, developing oral language and comprehension is also important when learning to read.

6

Point to the bold words in the sentence and ask your child to find all the "b" letters. The words with the "b" letters are in bold to make it easier. They can't read these sentences yet. This is just to help them recognize what the letter looks like—and pick it out from a word. It may not be easy for them.

7

Read each sound slowly. The sound buttons under the letters tell you if the sounds are made up of one or more letters. In this image, "r-u-b" are all individual sounds. In other words, such as "care," the sound "are" is represented by three letters, but it is still a single sound. Ask your child to say the separate sounds slowly. Then say them again faster. Finally, blend the sounds together to make the word.

8

Trace the letter, first with a finger and then with a pencil. After your child has traced the letter three times, ask them to try writing the letter twice. This will really help them with handwriting later. When they have done this, practice reading the sounds and blending the word together again.

9

Here is a chance for your child to try writing the letter themselves. Starting at the correct point will really help. After they have traced the letter three times, ask them to try writing the letter twice. They should not worry if it doesn't look like the letter. It takes time to get this right.

10

These are words that your child can now try to read. With each word, they should first sound out the letters, then blend the sounds to read.

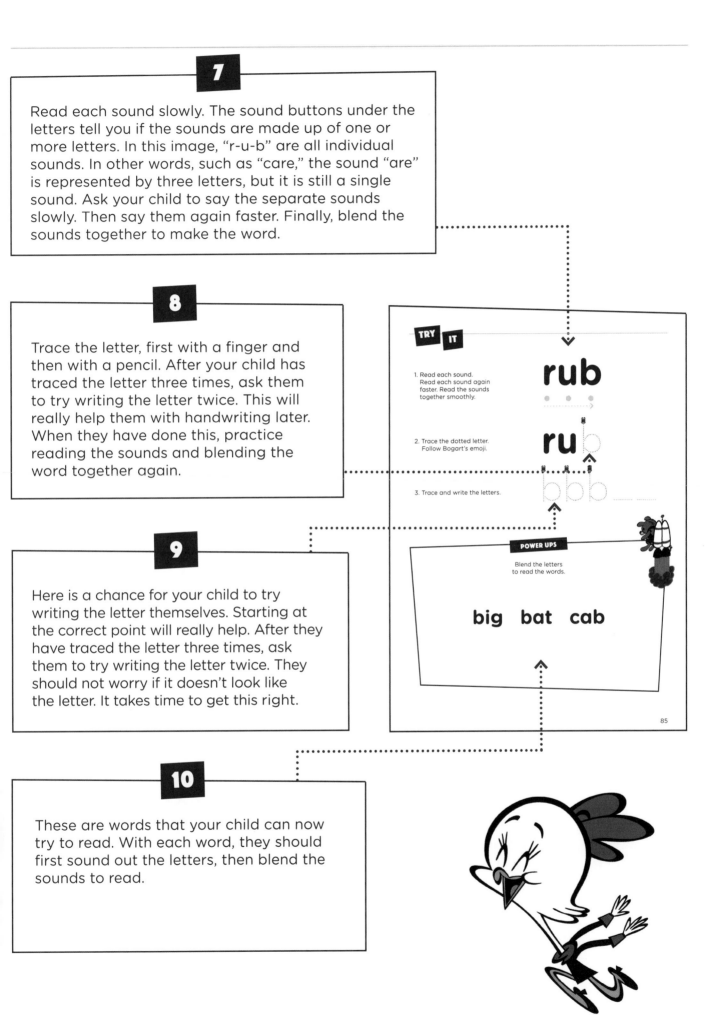

TRY IT

1. Read each sound. Read each sound again faster. Read the sounds together smoothly.

rub

2. Trace the dotted letter. Follow Bogart's emoji.

ru b

3. Trace and write the letters.

b b b

POWER UPS

Blend the letters to read the words.

big   bat   cab

85

can you say?

S

sat

S	s
upper case	lower case

FIND IT

Can you find the letters for the **s** sound that are in the words in bold? Circle them.

Bearnice **sat** on top of Brick. "Go **faster**!" she **said**.

sat

1. Read each sound.
   Read each sound again
   faster. Read the sounds
   together smoothly.

sat

2. Trace the dotted letter.
   Follow Bogart's emoji.

sss _____ _____

3. Trace and write the letters.

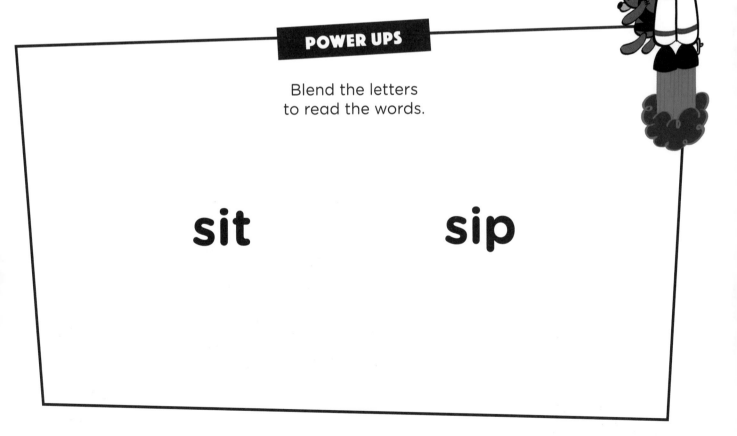

POWER UPS

Blend the letters
to read the words.

sit

sip

can you say?

a

ant

A
upper case

a
lower case

FIND IT

Can you find the letters for the **a** sound that are in the words in bold? Circle them.

Barksy **had ants** in her **pants**.

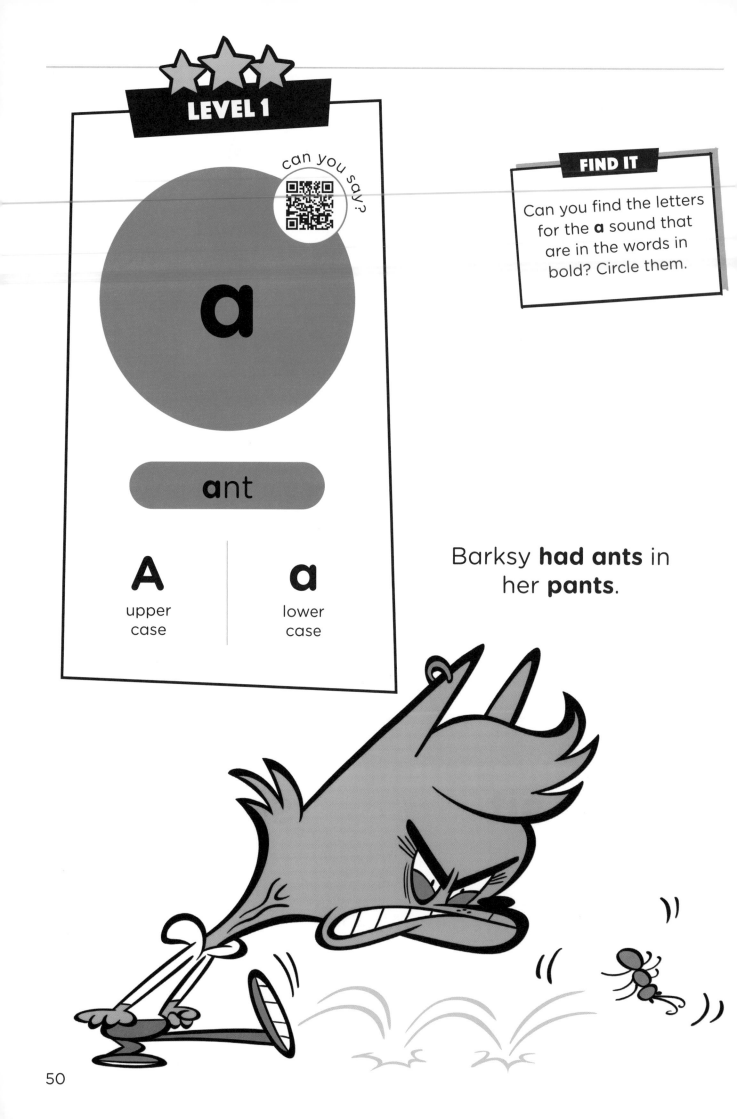

1. Read each sound.
   Read each sound again
   faster. Read the sounds
   together smoothly.

ant

2. Trace the dotted letter.
   Follow Bogart's emoji.

nt

3. Trace and write the letters.

a a a _____ _____

POWER UPS

Blend the letters
to read the words.

at   **pan**

can you say?

t

tap

T
upper case

t
lower case

Turn on the **water tap**, **Grit**!

1. Read each sound.
   Read each sound again
   faster. Read the sounds
   together smoothly.

tap

2. Trace the dotted letter.
   Follow Bogart's emoji.

ap

3. Trace and write the letters.

POWER UPS

Blend the letters
to read the words.

tan   tin

can you say?

p

pat

P	p
upper case	lower case

FIND IT

Can you find the letters for the **p** sound that are in the words in bold? Circle them.

"Good **pup**!" said Bearnice. She likes to **pat** her **pup** on **top** of his head.

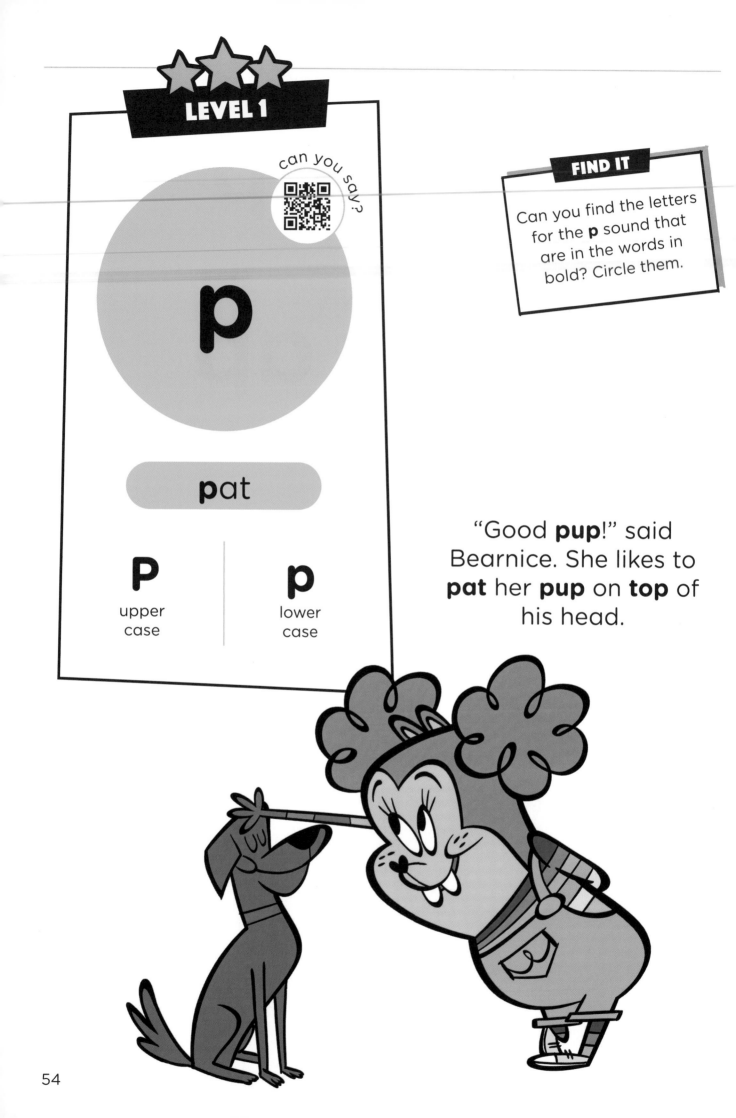

1. Read each sound.
   Read each sound again
   faster. Read the sounds
   together smoothly.

pat

2. Trace the dotted letter.
   Follow Bogart's emoji.

pat

3. Trace and write the letters.

ppp _____ _____

POWER UPS

Blend the letters
to read the words.

nip   tip

can you say?

i

sip

I
upper
case

i
lower
case

FIND IT

Can you find the letters for the **i** sound that are in the words in bold? Circle them.

Oz sat on the chair and **sipped** a hot **drink**.

1. Read each sound.
   Read each sound again
   faster. Read the sounds
   together smoothly.

sip

2. Trace the dotted letter.
   Follow Bogart's emoji.

s i p

3. Trace and write the letters.

POWER UPS

Blend the letters
to read the words.

nip   **tip**

can you say?

Can you find the letters for the **n** sound that are in the words in bold? Circle them.

n

nap

N
upper case

n
lower case

Brick took a **nap under** the tree.

1. Read each sound.
   Read each sound again
   faster. Read the sounds
   together smoothly.

nap

2. Trace the dotted letter.
   Follow Bogart's emoji.

nap

3. Trace and write the letters.

nnn _____ _____

POWER UPS

Blend the letters
to read the words.

an   pin

can you say?

m

map

M
upper case

m
lower case

Can you find the letters for the **m** sound that are in the words in bold? Circle them.

"Follow **me**," said Grit. "I have a **map**."

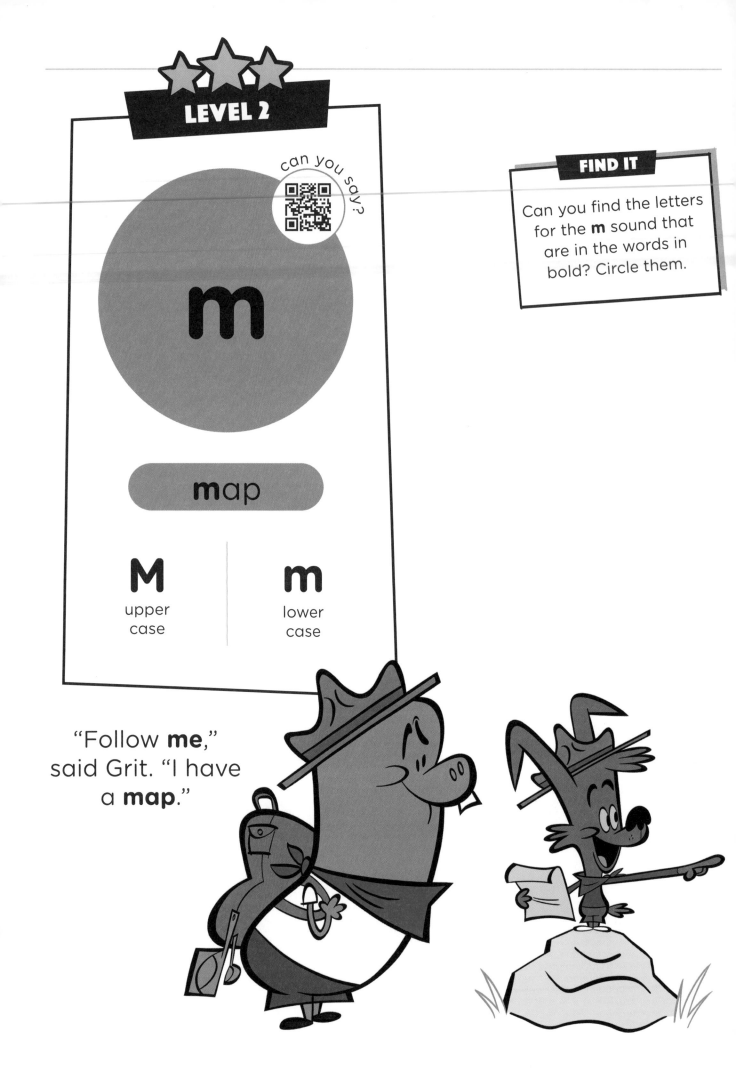

1. Read each sound.
   Read each sound again
   faster. Read the sounds
   together smoothly.

map

2. Trace the dotted letter.
   Follow Bogart's emoji.

map

3. Trace and write the letters.

POWER UPS

Blend the letters
to read the words.

man   mat

can you say?

d

sa**d**

D
upper case

d
lower case

FIND IT

Can you find the letters for the **d** sound that are in the words in bold? Circle them.

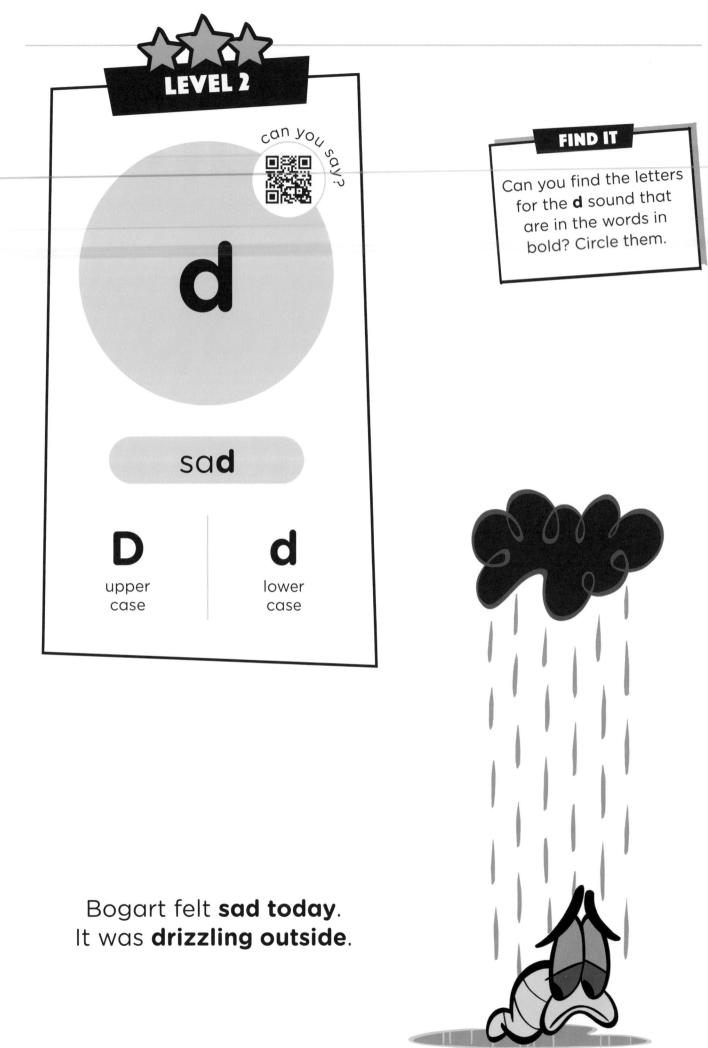

Bogart felt **sad today**.
It was **drizzling outside**.

1. Read each sound.
   Read each sound again
   faster. Read the sounds
   together smoothly.

sad

2. Trace the dotted letter.
   Follow Bogart's emoji.

sad

3. Trace and write the letters.

dad

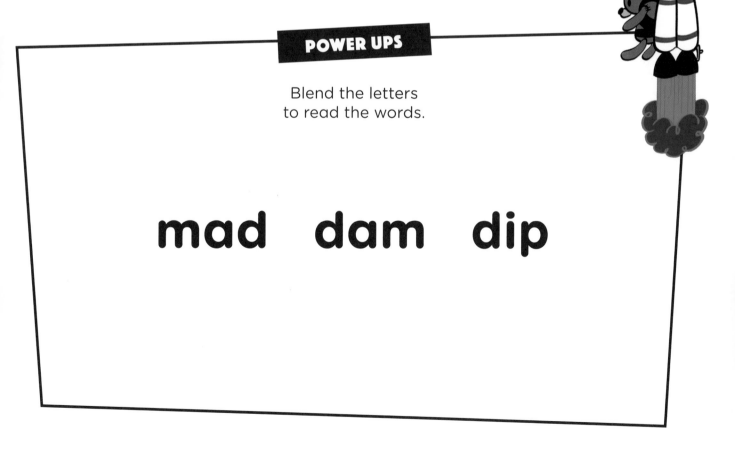

POWER UPS

Blend the letters
to read the words.

mad   dam   dip

can you say?

Can you find the letters for the **o** sound that are in the words in bold? Circle them.

O

p o t

O
upper case

O
lower case

The **pot on** the table is empty.

pot
• • •

1. Read each sound.
   Read each sound again
   faster. Read the sounds
   together smoothly.

pot

2. Trace the dotted letter.
   Follow Bogart's emoji.

3. Trace and write the letters.

POWER UPS

Blend the letters
to read the words.

on   top   hot

65

can you say?

FIND IT

Can you find the letters for the **g** sound that are in the words in bold? Circle them.

g

dog

G
upper case

g
lower case

Grit the **dog** chased his tail.

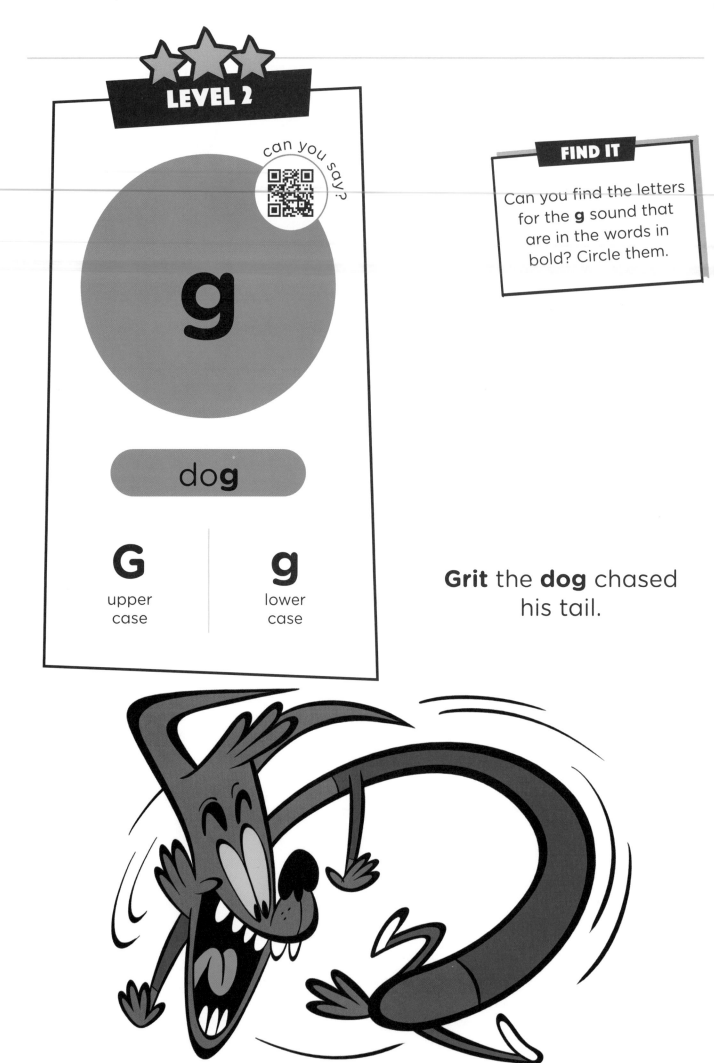

1. Read each sound.
   Read each sound again
   faster. Read the sounds
   together smoothly.

dog

2. Trace the dotted letter.
   Follow Bogart's emoji.

3. Trace and write the letters.

POWER UPS

Blend the letters
to read the words.

dig tag gas

can you say?

C

cat

C
upper case

c
lower case

FIND IT

Can you find the letters for the **c** sound that are in the words in bold? Circle them.

The **cats** drew a **cool picture** in the sand.

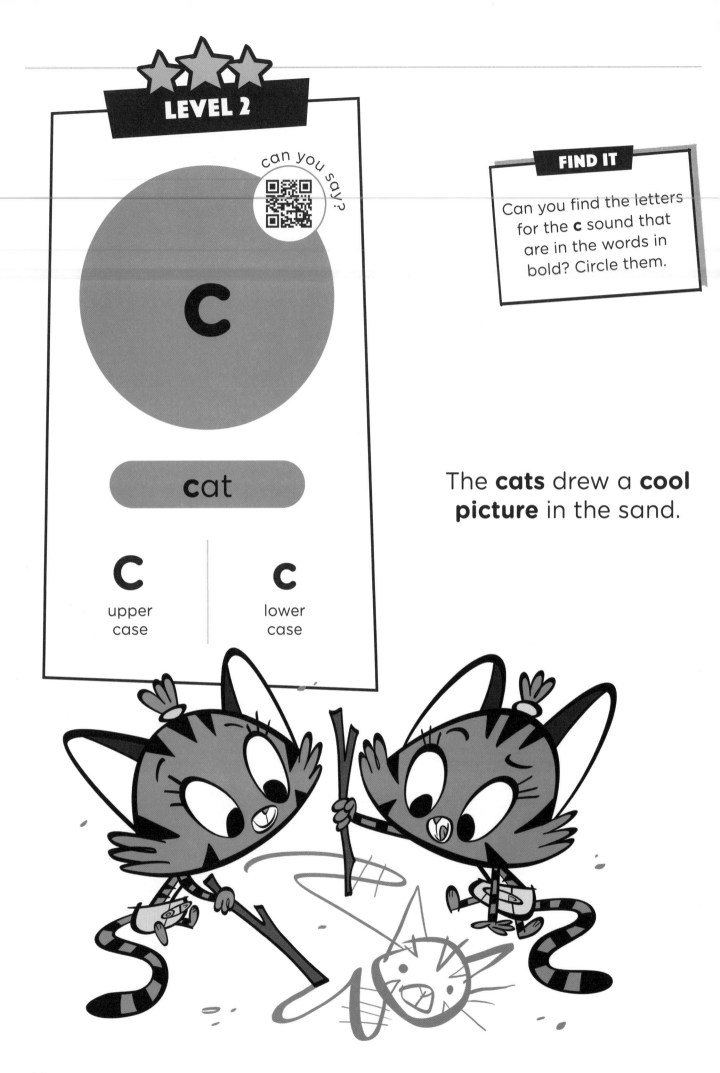

1. Read each sound. Read each sound again faster. Read the sounds together smoothly.

cat

2. Trace the dotted letter. Follow Bogart's emoji.

cat

3. Trace and write the letters.

c c c _____ _____

POWER UPS

Blend the letters to read the words.

can   cap   cot

can you say?

k

kit

K

upper case

Remember! The same sound can be represented in different ways.

Can you find the letters for the **k** sound that are in the words in bold? Circle them.

"Do you have a first aid **kit** for **kids**?" Grit **asked**.

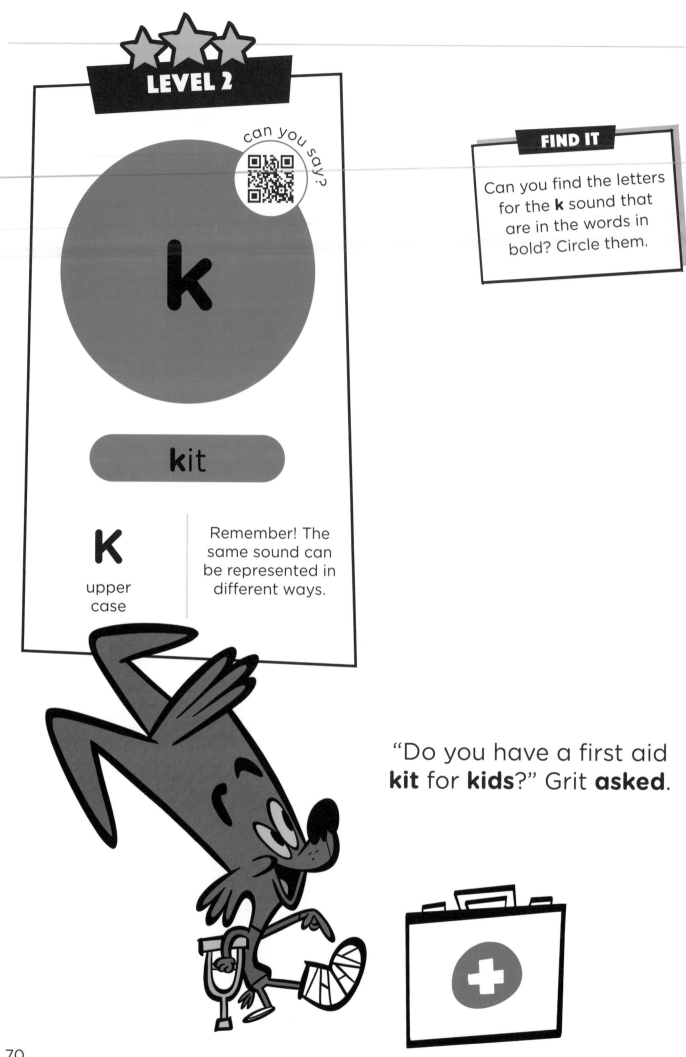

TRY **IT**

1. Read each sound.
   Read each sound again
   faster. Read the sounds
   together smoothly.

kit

2. Trace the dotted letter.
   Follow Bogart's emoji.

kit

3. Trace and write the letters.

kkk _____ _____

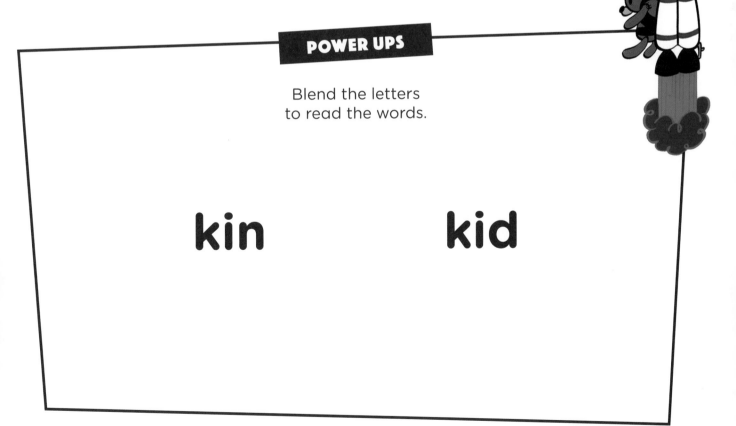

POWER UPS

Blend the letters
to read the words.

kin   kid

can you say?

ck

kick

CK
upper case

Remember! A single sound can be represented by two letters.

Can you find the letters for the **ck** sound that are in the words in bold? Circle them.

Bearnice **kicked** the ball into the sky.

Thwack!

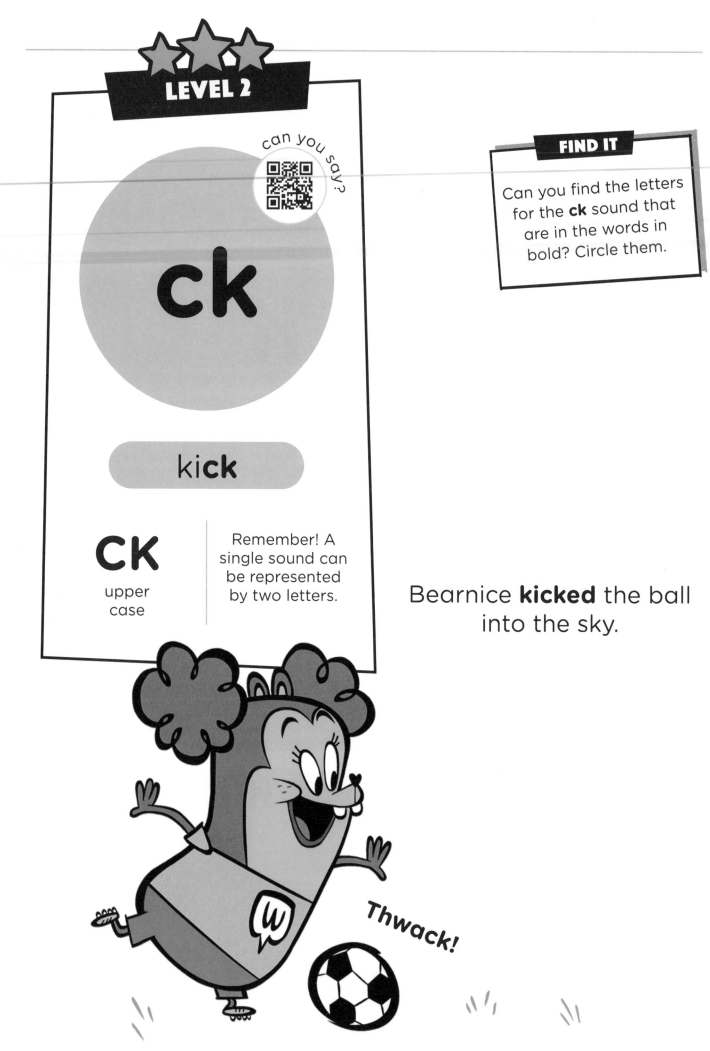

1. Read each sound.
   Read each sound again
   faster. Read the sounds
   together smoothly.

kick

2. Trace the dotted letter.
   Follow Bogart's emoji.

ki ck

3. Trace and write the letters.

ck

POWER UPS

Blend the letters
to read the words.

pick sick sock

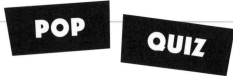

Practice the words you learned in Level 2.

map

man

mat

sad

mad

dam

dip

dog

dig

tag

gas

pot

on

top

can

cap

cot

kit

kin

kid

You've got this!

Try these harder words with consonant clusters (two or more consonants side by side). You can do it! You have learned all the sounds.

You can do it!

mint

damp

sand

gap

pig

stop

act

camp

skin

snack

stick

can you say?

Can you find the letters for the **e** sound that are in the words in bold? Circle them.

e

net

E
upper case

e
lower case

Let's use a **net** to catch a **yellow** star!

net

1. Read each sound.
   Read each sound again
   faster. Read the sounds
   together smoothly.

nt

2. Trace the dotted letter.
   Follow Bogart's emoji.

3. Trace and write the letters.

POWER UPS

Blend the letters
to read the words.

ten   met   get

can you say?

u

mud

U
upper case

u
lower case

Can you find the letters for the **u** sound that are in the words in bold? Circle them.

Yin **jumped up** and down in the **mud**.

1. Read each sound.
   Read each sound again
   faster. Read the sounds
   together smoothly.

mud

2. Trace the dotted letter.
   Follow Bogart's emoji.

mud

3. Trace and write the letters.

POWER UPS

Blend the letters
to read the words.

cut nut sun

can you say?

r

rock

R
upper case

r
lower case

Can you find the letters for the **r** sound that are in the words in bold? Circle them.

Shang High **dropped** the **rock right** on his big toe!

1. Read each sound.
   Read each sound again
   faster. Read the sounds
   together smoothly.

rock

2. Trace the dotted letter.
   Follow Bogart's emoji.

rock

3. Trace and write the letters.

POWER UPS

Blend the letters
to read the words.

run   red   rat

can you say?

h

hat

H	**h**
upper case	lower case

Can you find the letters for the **h** sound that are in the words in bold? Circle them.

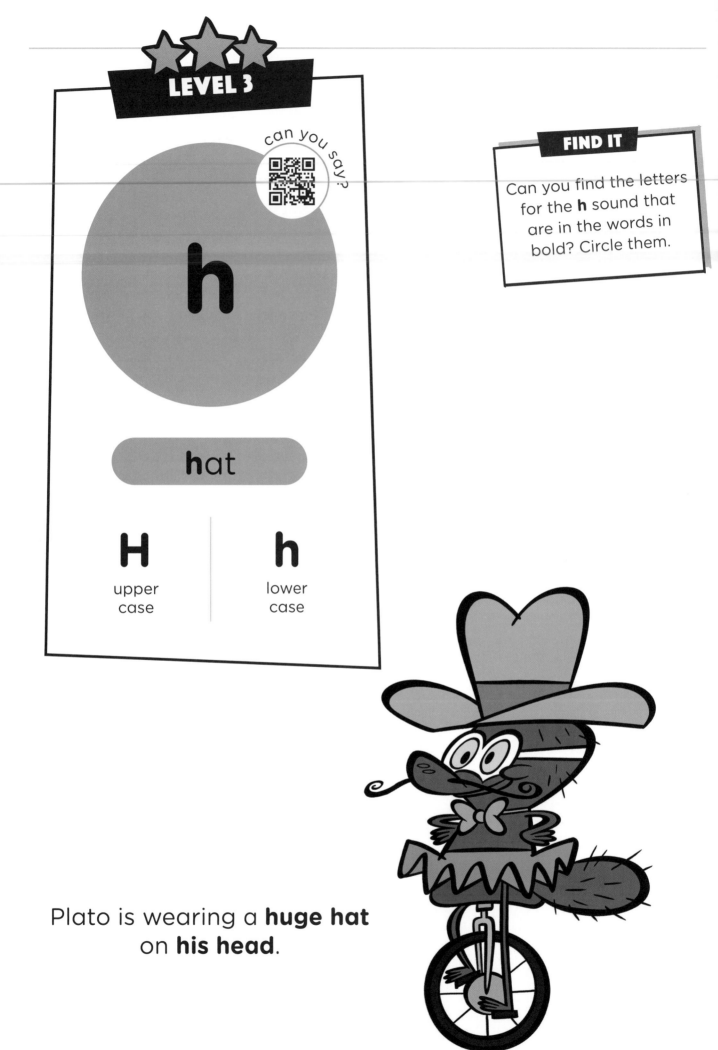

Plato is wearing a **huge hat** on **his head**.

1. Read each sound.
   Read each sound again
   faster. Read the sounds
   together smoothly.

hat

2. Trace the dotted letter.
   Follow Bogart's emoji.

at

3. Trace and write the letters.

POWER UPS

Blend the letters
to read the words.

hug   him   hit

can you say?

b

rub

B
upper case

b
lower case

FIND IT

Can you find the letters for the **b** sound that are in the words in bold? Circle them.

Rub a **dub dub**. The **big brush scrubbed** Yang from side to side.

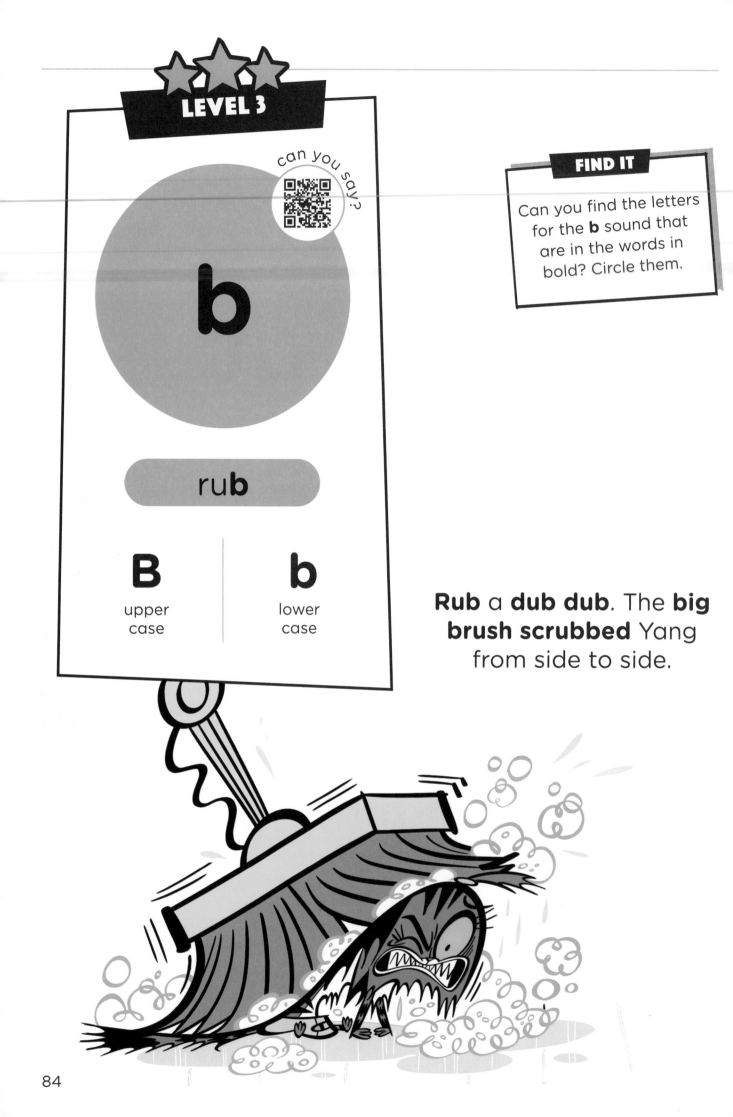

1. Read each sound.
   Read each sound again
   faster. Read the sounds
   together smoothly.

2. Trace the dotted letter.
   Follow Bogart's emoji.

3. Trace and write the letters.

POWER UPS

Blend the letters
to read the words.

big bat cab

can you say?

f

fib

F
upper case

f
lower case

FIND IT

Can you find the letters for the **f** sound that are in the words in bold? Circle them.

Armie told a **fib** about a **fight** with a big **fish**.

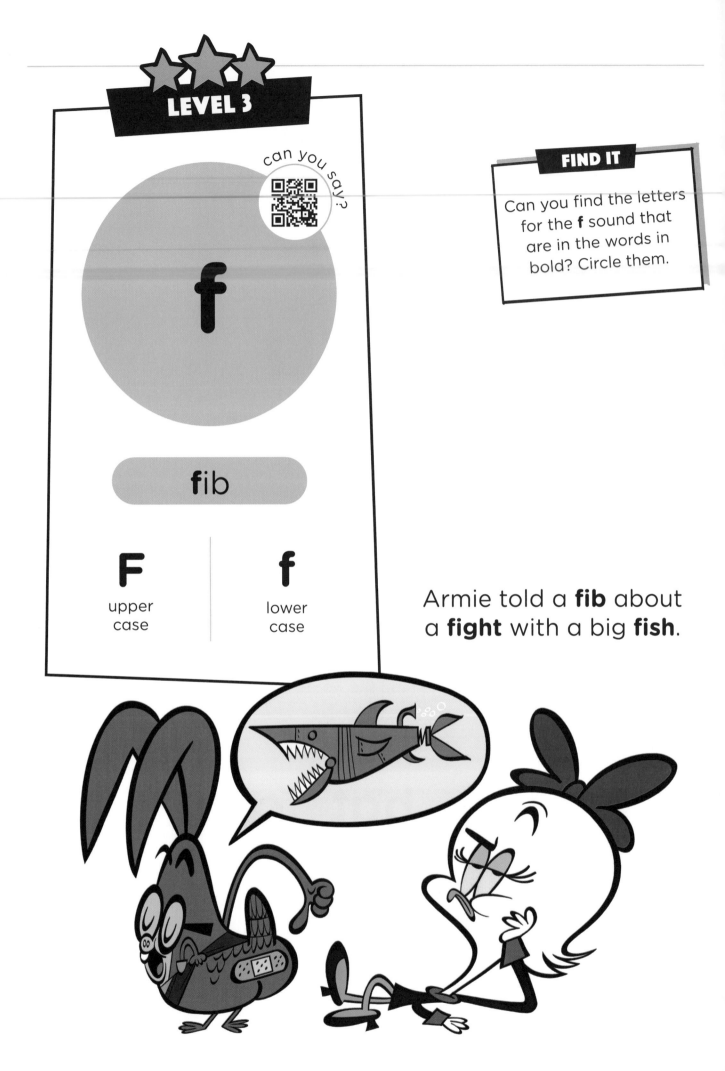

fib

1. Read each sound. Read each sound again faster. Read the sounds together smoothly.

fib

2. Trace the dotted letter. Follow Bogart's emoji.

fff

3. Trace and write the letters.

Blend the letters
to read the words.

fun   fit   fed

can you say?

ff

puff

FF

upper case

Remember! A single sound can be represented by two letters.

Can you find the letters for the **ff** sound that are in the words in bold? Circle them.

The **giraffe huffed** and **puffed** until he blew out all the candles.

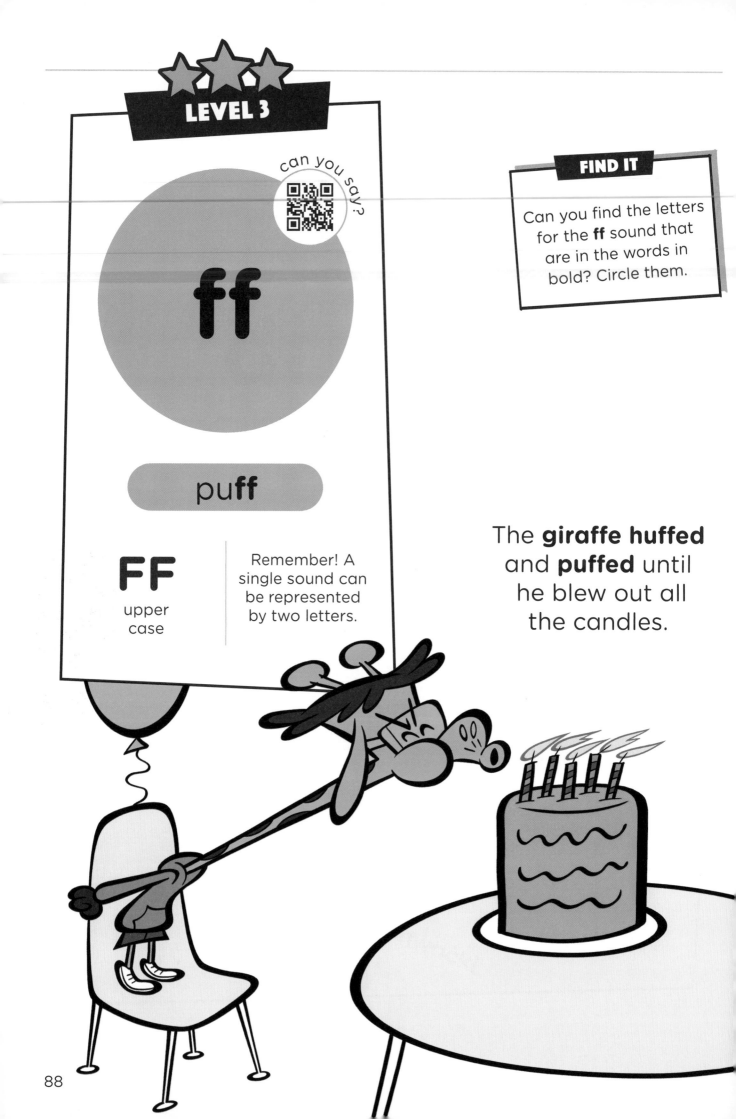

1. Read each sound.
   Read each sound again
   faster. Read the sounds
   together smoothly.

puff

2. Trace the dotted letter.
   Follow Bogart's emoji.

puff

ff

3. Trace and write the letters.

POWER UPS

Blend the letters
to read the words.

off   huff   sniff

can you say?

lift

L
upper case

I
lower case

Can you find the letters for the **l** sound that are in the words in bold? Circle them.

Shang High **lifted** the rock and found a **little** worm.

"Hi, Bogart!"

lift

1. Read each sound.
   Read each sound again
   faster. Read the sounds
   together smoothly.

ift

2. Trace the dotted letter.
   Follow Bogart's emoji.

3. Trace and write the letters.

POWER UPS

Blend the letters
to read the words.

lip lot leg

can you say?

ll

smell

LL
upper case

ll
lower case

FIND IT

Can you find the letters for the **ll** sound that are in the words in bold? Circle them.

Brick **fell** in love with the **smell** of **all** the flowers.

1. Read each sound.
   Read each sound again
   faster. Read the sounds
   together smoothly.

smell

2. Trace the dotted letter.
   Follow Bogart's emoji.

sme

3. Trace and write the letters.

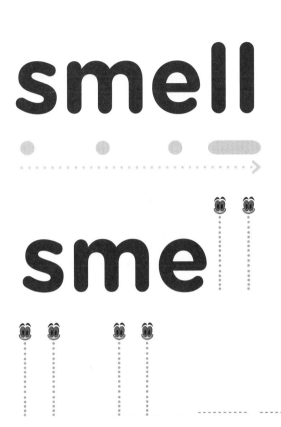

POWER UPS

Blend the letters
to read the words.

tell pill bell

can you say?

ss

me**ss**

SS
upper case

ss
lower case

Can you find the letters for the **ss** sound that are in the words in bold? Circle them.

Grit was very **stressed** about cleaning up his **mess**.

1. Read each sound.
   Read each sound again
   faster. Read the sounds
   together smoothly.

mess

2. Trace the dotted letter.
   Follow Bogart's emoji.

me ss

3. Trace and write the letters.

ss _____ _____

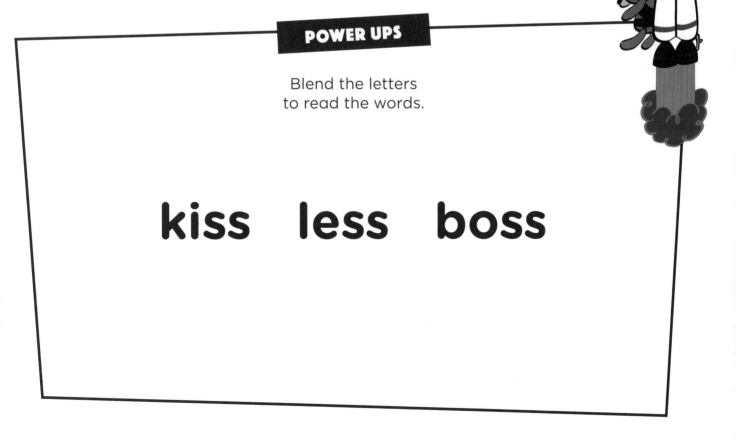

POWER UPS

Blend the letters
to read the words.

kiss   less   boss

Practice the words you learned in Level 3.

You've got this!

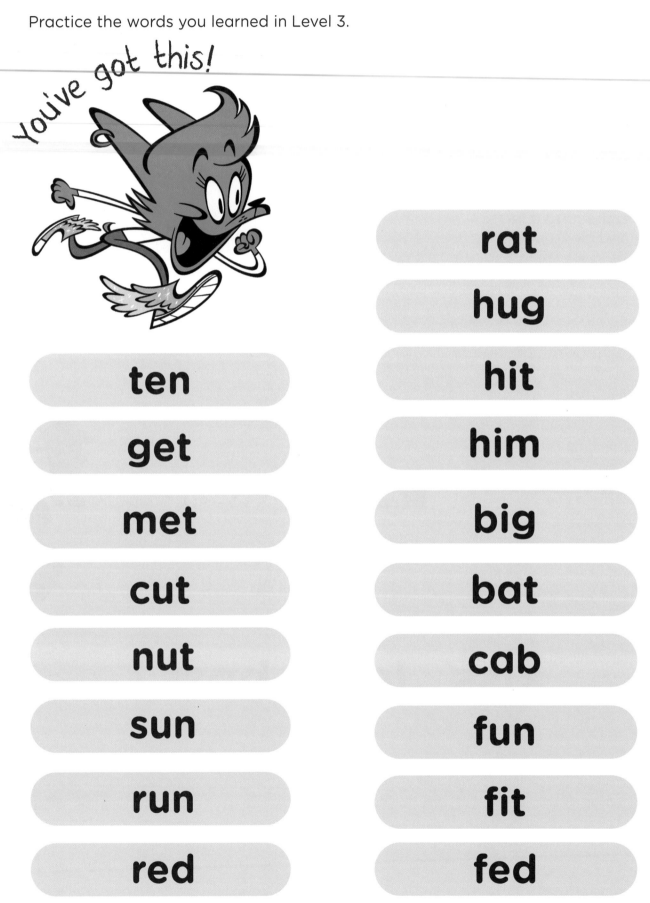

ten

get

met

cut

nut

sun

run

red

rat

hug

hit

him

big

bat

cab

fun

fit

fed

Try these harder words with consonant clusters (two or more consonants side by side). You can do it! You have learned all the sounds.

tent

bed

bend

rest

mug

truck

hand

bus

bad

best

muffin

left

help

luck

sell

You can do it!

97

can you say?

j

jump

J	j
upper case	lower case

Oz **jumped** for **joy**. She **just** felt so happy.

1. Read each sound. Read each sound again faster. Read the sounds together smoothly.

jump

2. Trace the dotted letter. Follow Bogart's emoji.

jump

3. Trace and write the letters.

j j j

POWER UPS

Blend the letters to read the words.

jog   jam   jet

can you say?

V

van

V
upper case

v
lower case

FIND IT

Can you find the letters for the **v** sound that are in the words in bold? Circle them.

Vroom! Vroom! The noisy **van drove** away **very** quickly.

PLATO'S

TACOS

PT

PT

TAC01

1. Read each sound.
   Read each sound again
   faster. Read the sounds
   together smoothly.

van

2. Trace the dotted letter.
   Follow Bogart's emoji.

van

3. Trace and write the letters.

POWER UPS

Blend the letters
to read the words.

vet   vat

can you say?

W

wet

W
upper case

W
lower case

FIND IT

Can you find the letters for the **w** sound that are in the words in bold? Circle them.

Grit sprayed **water** on Plato's face.

Plato did not **want** to get **wet**!

1. Read each sound. Read each sound again faster. Read the sounds together smoothly.

wet

2. Trace the dotted letter. Follow Bogart's emoji.

wet

3. Trace and write the letters.

w w _____ _____

 **POWER UPS**

Blend the letters to read the words.

will   web

can you say?

FIND IT

Can you find the letters for the **x** sound that are in the words in bold? Circle them.

X

fi**x**

X
upper case

X
lower case

"Relax," said Yin.

"We can **fix** it! All we need is some **extra**-strong glue."

fix

1. Read each sound.
Read each sound again
faster. Read the sounds
together smoothly.

2. Trace the dotted letter.
Follow Bogart's emoji.

3. Trace and write the letters.

POWER UPS

Blend the letters
to read the words.

box   fox   six

can you say?

y

yell

Y	**y**
upper case	lower case

FIND IT

Can you find the letters for the **y** sound that are in the words in bold? Circle them.

"**Yes**, okay! **You** don't need to shout!" Plato said.

Grit should not **yell** at Plato.

yell

1. Read each sound. Read each sound again faster. Read the sounds together smoothly.

2. Trace the dotted letter. Follow Bogart's emoji.

yell

3. Trace and write the letters.

POWER UPS

Blend the letters to read the words.

yes   **yap**

can you say?

z

zip

Z
upper case

z
lower case

FIND IT

Can you find the letters for the **z** sound that are in the words in bold? Circle them.

"Your mouth is **zipped**!" cried Armie.
"I will **unzip** it!"

1. Read each sound.
   Read each sound again
   faster. Read the sounds
   together smoothly.

2. Trace the dotted letter.
   Follow Bogart's emoji.

3. Trace and write the letters.

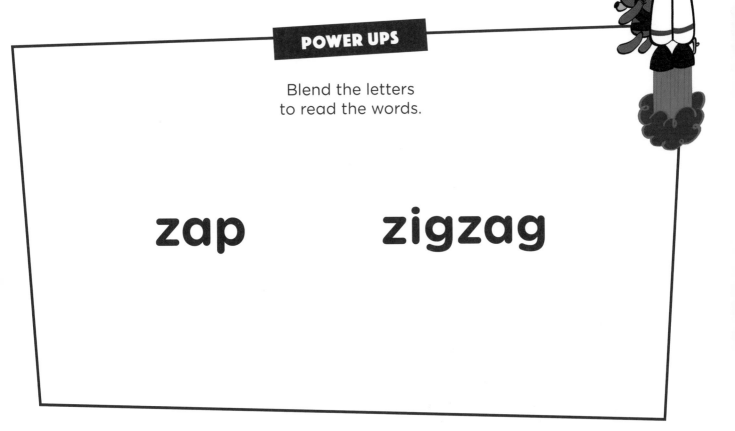

POWER UPS

Blend the letters
to read the words.

zap   **zigzag**

can you say?

zz

bu**zz**

ZZ
upper case

zz
lower case

FIND IT

Can you find the letters for the **zz** sound that are in the words in bold? Circle them.

The bees **buzzed** as they **whizzed** through **dazzling** sunshine.

1. Read each sound.
   Read each sound again
   faster. Read the sounds
   together smoothly.

buzz

2. Trace the dotted letter.
   Follow Bogart's emoji.

buzz

3. Trace and write the letters.

POWER UPS

Blend the letters
to read the words.

fizz fuzz jazz

can you say?

sh

flush

SH
upper case

sh
lower case

FIND IT

Can you find the letters for the **sh** sound that are in the words in bold? Circle them.

"Don't forget to **flush** the toilet!" **shouted** Oz.

"**Shoo shoo**, little poo!"

1. Read each sound. Read each sound again faster. Read the sounds together smoothly.

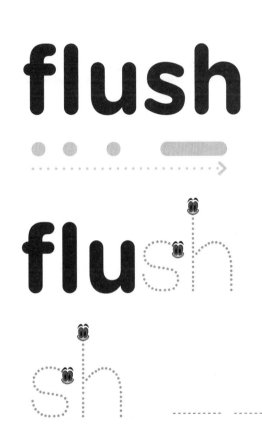

flush

2. Trace the dotted letter. Follow Bogart's emoji.

3. Trace and write the letters.

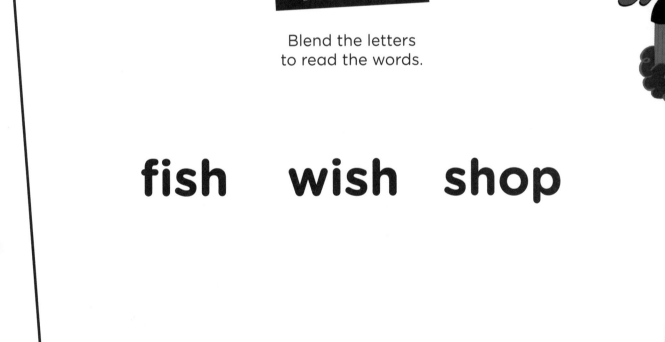

POWER UPS

Blend the letters to read the words.

fish   wish   shop

can you say?

ch

chat

CH
upper case

ch
lower case

FIND IT

Can you find the letters for the **ch** sound that are in the words in bold? Circle them.

"**Cheer** up!" **chuckled** Plato.

"We can **chat** on the phone until you feel better."

TRY IT

1. Read each sound.
Read each sound again faster. Read the sounds together smoothly.

chat

2. Trace the dotted letter.
Follow Bogart's emoji.

ch at

3. Trace and write the letters.

ch

POWER UPS

Blend the letters to read the words.

chop   chin   rich

can you say?

th

thick

TH	th
upper case	lower case

FIND IT

Can you find the letters for the **th** sound that are in the words in bold? Circle them.

Yang drew a **thin** line

and Yin drew a **thick** line.

1. Read each sound.
   Read each sound again faster. Read the sounds together smoothly.

thick

2. Trace the dotted letter. Follow Bogart's emoji.

th**ick**

3. Trace and write the letters.

th

POWER UPS

Blend the letters to read the words.

moth   thin   cloth

CVC a
BUBBLE BATH

Can you make three CVC (consonant vowel consonant) words like "c-a-t"? Choose a beginning consonant and an ending consonant and write them in the CVC bubbles. Draw some more bubbles and make more CVC words!

BEGINNING
CONSONANTS

b c d
f g h
j l m
n p r
s t v
w y

a

a

a

ENDING
CONSONANTS

b d g
m n p
t

CVC e
BUBBLE BATH

e

e

e

BEGINNING CONSONANTS

b d f
g h j
l m n
p r s
t v w
y

ENDING CONSONANTS

d g n
t

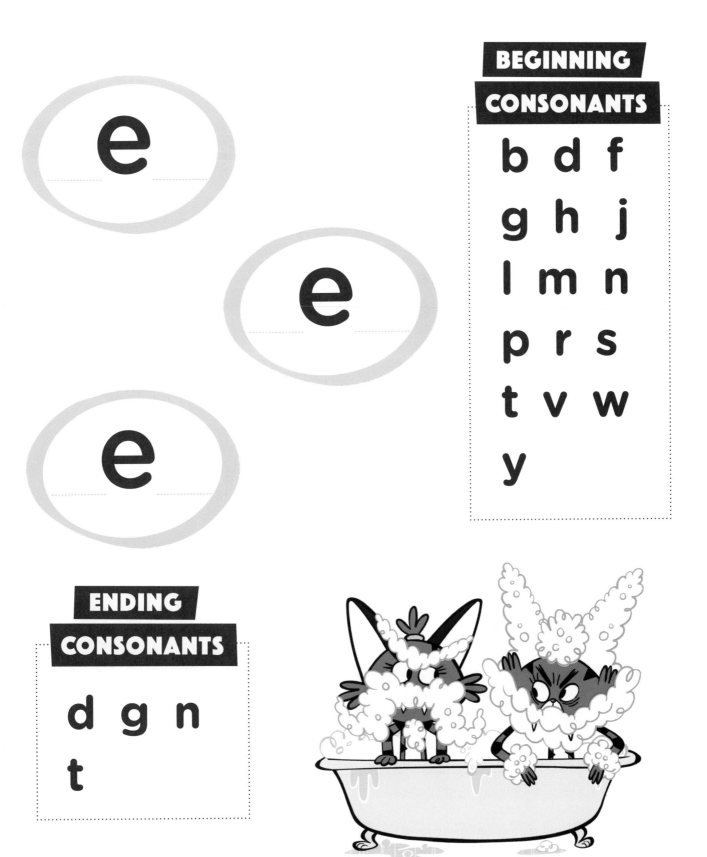

119

CVC i
BUBBLE BATH

Can you make three CVC (consonant vowel consonant) words like "s-i-t"? Choose a beginning consonant and an ending consonant and write them in the CVC bubbles. Draw some more bubbles and make more CVC words!

BEGINNING CONSONANTS

b d f
g h j
k l m
n p r
s t v
w y z

i

i

i

ENDING CONSONANTS

d g m
n p t

CVC O
BUBBLE BATH

O

O

O

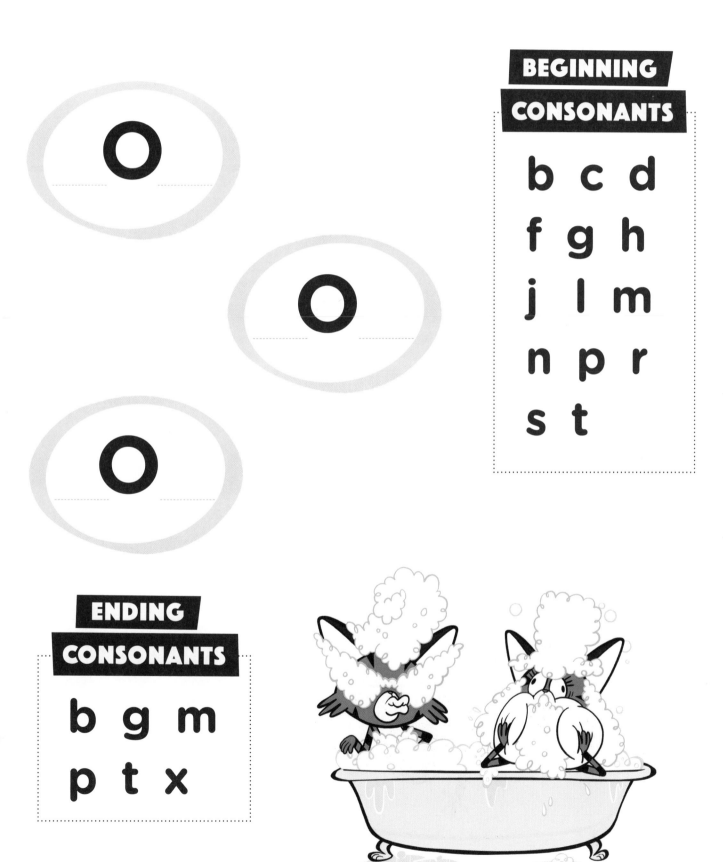

BEGINNING CONSONANTS

b c d
f g h
j l m
n p r
s t

ENDING CONSONANTS

b g m
p t x

121

CVC U
BUBBLE BATH

Can you make three CVC (consonant vowel consonant) words like "s-u-n"? Choose a beginning consonant and an ending consonant and write them in the CVC bubbles. Draw some more bubbles and make more CVC words!

BEGINNING CONSONANTS

b c d
f g h
j l m
n p r
s t

u

u

u

ENDING CONSONANTS

b d g
m n p
t s

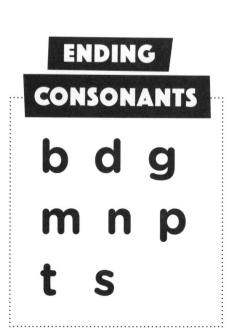

DIGRAPHS: DOUBLE LETTERS

When two letters come together to make one sound, they are called a **digraph**.

Some words end with the double letters "**ss**," "**ll**," "**ff**," "**zz**," "**ck**."

Circle the word that matches the picture.

1. (kiss)   puff

2. fill   bell

3. buzz   sniff

4. duck   sell

5. mess   back

6. dress   less

SHORT VOWELS: COMPLETE THE WORDS

Complete these words with the correct short vowel to make a real word.

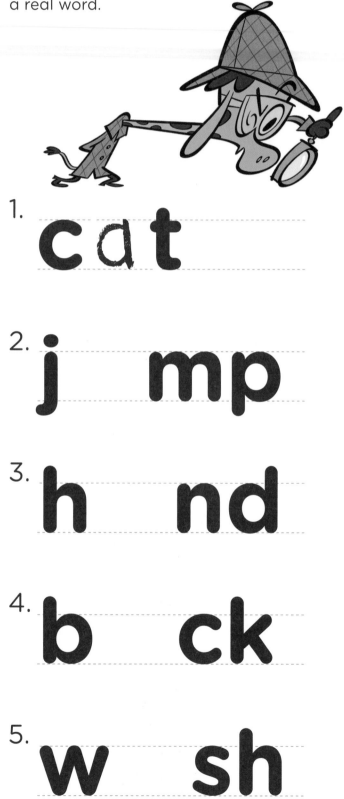

1. c a t

2. j _ mp

3. h _ nd

4. b _ ck

5. w _ sh

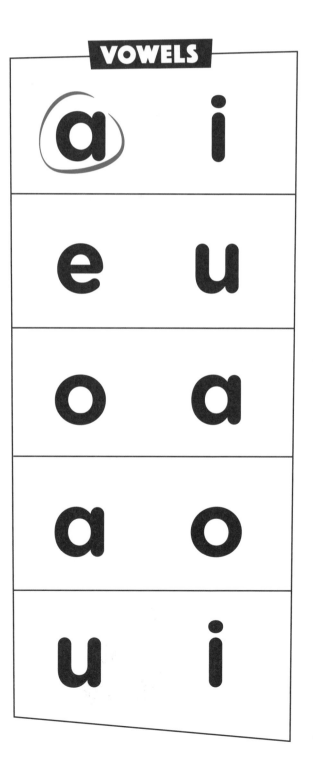

VOWELS

(a)	i
e	u
o	a
a	o
u	i

Vowel sounds can be long or short.

The sound of **a** in **apple** is a short vowel sound.
The sound of **ai** in **rain** is a long vowel sound.

VOWELS

e	u
o	a
a	i
e	i
u	e

6. r ___ d

7. b ___ x

8. f ___ sh

9. ___ gg

10. b ___ s

PHONICS:
SOUND BUTTONS &
READING PRACTICE

INSTRUCTIONS:

1. Sound button the words.

When a single letter (grapheme) makes one sound (phoneme), put a **dot** under it.

cat
• • •

2. Blend and read the words.

1.	**cat**	2.	**run**
3.	**gap**	4.	**mop**
5.	**fun**	6.	**sit**
7.	**pot**	8.	**net**
9.	**wig**	10.	**fox**

11.   **sad**   12.   **hat**

13.   **wet**   14.   **mud**

15.   **lip**   16.   **dog**

17.   **zip**   18.   **box**

Try to decode these nonreal words in the same way.

19.   **bab**   20.   **gab**

21.   **beb**   22.   **cag**

PHONICS:
SOUND BUTTONS & READING PRACTICE

1. Sound button the words.

> When a single letter (grapheme) makes one sound (phoneme), put a **dot** under it.
>
> **cat**
> • • •

2. Blend and read the words.

3. Real or not real?

> On this page, there are words that are real and words that are not real. You have to decide which is which.
>
> Check the box if the word is **real**.
>
> **cat** ✓   **pag** ☐
> • • •   • • •

1. **pin** ☐   2. **dim** ☐

3. **hig** ☐   4. **fim** ☐

5. **mub** ☐   6. **bet** ☐

7. **tin** ☐   8. **men** ☐

9. **beg** ☐   10. **mab** ☐

11. **gel** ☐   12. **mup** ☐

13. **yes** ☐   14. **jub** ☐

15. **leg** ☐   16. **six** ☐

17. **tap** ☐   18. **dat** ☐

19. **mit** ☐   20. **bag** ☐

PHONICS:
SOUND BUTTONS &
READING PRACTICE

INSTRUCTIONS:

1. Sound button the words.

When a single letter (grapheme) makes one sound (phoneme), put a **dot** under it.

cat
• • •

Spot the consonant teams (two letters that make one sound) and **underline** them.

chat
— • •

2. Blend and read the words.

1. **buzz**

2. **back**

3. **luck**

4. **chat**

5. **tell**

6. **rich**

7. **pick**

8. **shop**

9. **ship**   10. **miss**

11. **puff**   12. **chop**

13. **that**   14. **with**

15. **much**   16. **sack**

Try to decode these nonreal words in the same way.

17. **pezz**   18. **yich**

19. **kaff**   20. **tezz**

1. Sound button the words.

When a single letter (grapheme) makes one sound (phoneme), put a **dot** under it.

cat
• • •

Spot the consonant teams (two letters that make one sound) and **underline** them.

chat
— • •

2. Blend and read the words.

3. Real or not real?

On this page, there are words that are real and words that are not real. You have to decide which is which.

Check the box if the word is **real**.

cat ✓   **pag** ☐
• • •   • • •

1.	**hill**	☐	2.	**bell**	☐
3.	**yell**	☐	4.	**kezz**	☐
5.	**well**	☐	6.	**check**	☐
7.	**dull**	☐	8.	**moth**	☐

9. **jazz** ☐   10. **chill** ☐

11. **juck** ☐   12. **zoth** ☐

13. **coss** ☐   14. **shup** ☐

15. **chuck** ☐   16. **rell** ☐

17. **fizz** ☐   18. **bill** ☐

19. **rock** ☐   20. **shut** ☐

VOCABULARY

VOCABULARY

big

larger than normal

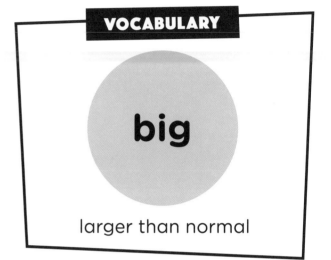

Circle the word that means the opposite of big.

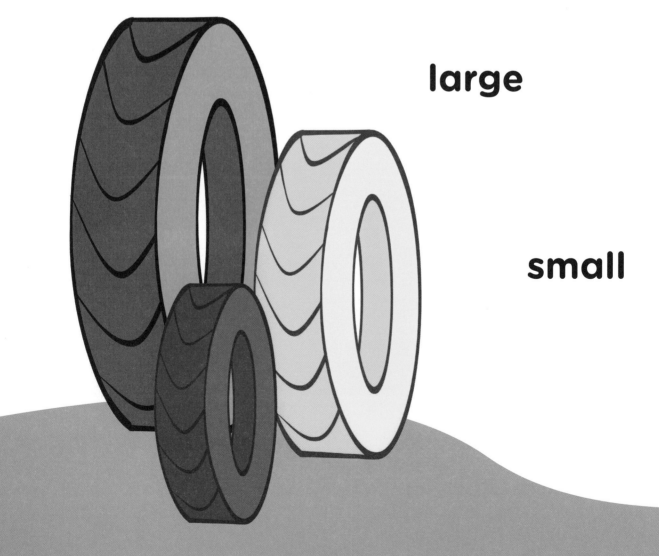

large

small

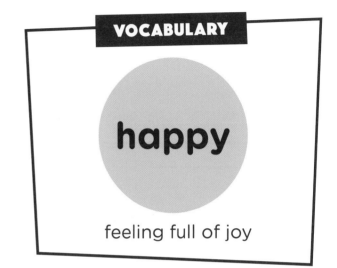

happy

feeling full of joy

Circle the word that means the opposite of happy.

sad

cheerful

PREPOSITIONS

Prepositions tell you where something is
or where something happens.

Write the prepositions next to the matching picture.

1.

on

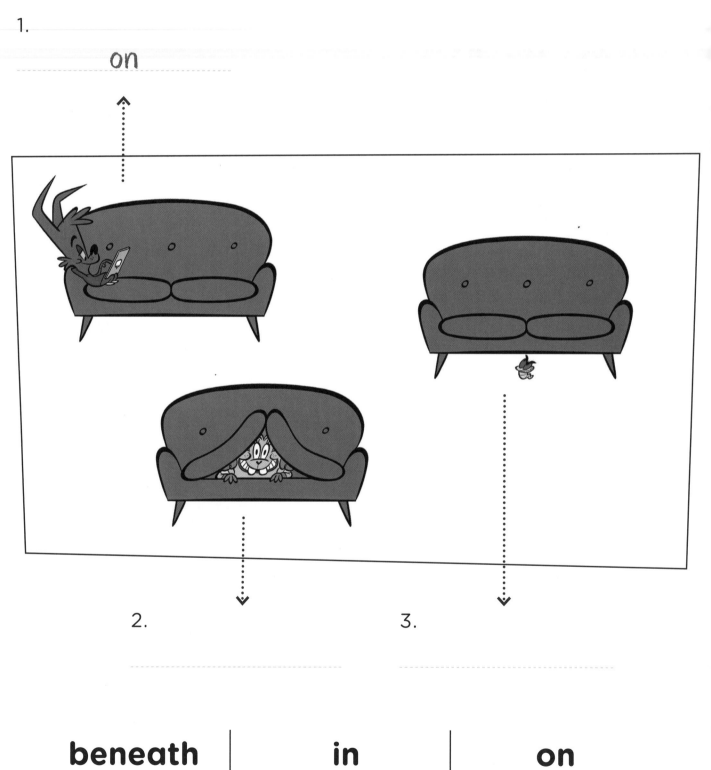

2.

3.

beneath | **in** | **on**

138

4.

5.

6.

in front of | **next to** | **behind**

Cause and effect show how two events are related. The second event (effect) happens as a result of the first event (cause).

CAUSE:

What happened first?

Draw what you think will happen as a result of the first image.

EFFECT:

What happened as a result?

CAUSE & EFFECT

Draw what you think happened first.

CAUSE:

What happened first?

Cause and effect show how two events are related.
The second event (effect) happens as a
result of the first event (cause).

What happened as a result?

CAUSE & EFFECT

Draw what you think happened first.

CAUSE:

What happened first?

Cause and effect show how two events are related.
The second event (effect) happens as a
result of the first event (cause).

What happened as a result?

SEQUENCING

Write **1** in the circle to show what happened **first**.
Write **2** in the circle to show what happened **next**.
Write **3** in the circle to show what happened **last**.

146

Can you retell this story?

Circle all the fruits.

Circle all the cars.

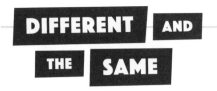

Which flowers are different, and which are the same?

Circle the flowers that are the same.

Draw a line from the emoji to the matching emotion.

| sad | laughing | angry | happy | crying |

1.

2.

3.

4.

5.

HIGH-FREQUENCY WORDS

HIGH-FREQUENCY WORDS

Use the paint-by-words chart to complete the picture. Use crayons, pencils, or paint!

ORANGE
it

BLUE
on

BROWN
is

GREEN
up

YELLOW
as

Use the paint-by-words chart to complete the picture and find the hidden words. Use crayons, pencils, or paint!

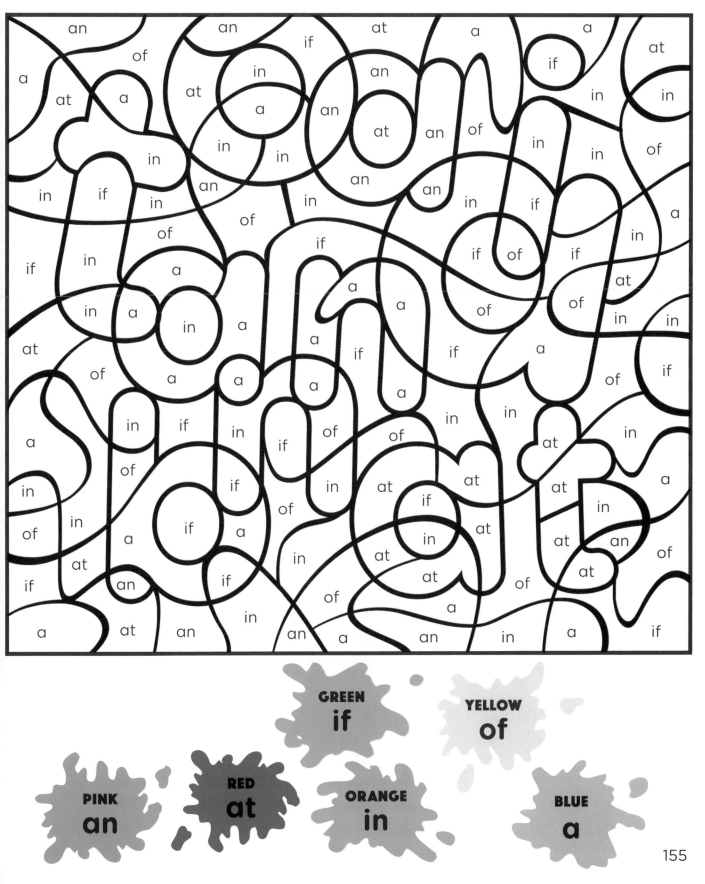

GREEN
if

YELLOW
of

PINK
an

RED
at

ORANGE
in

BLUE
a

HIGH-FREQUENCY WORDS

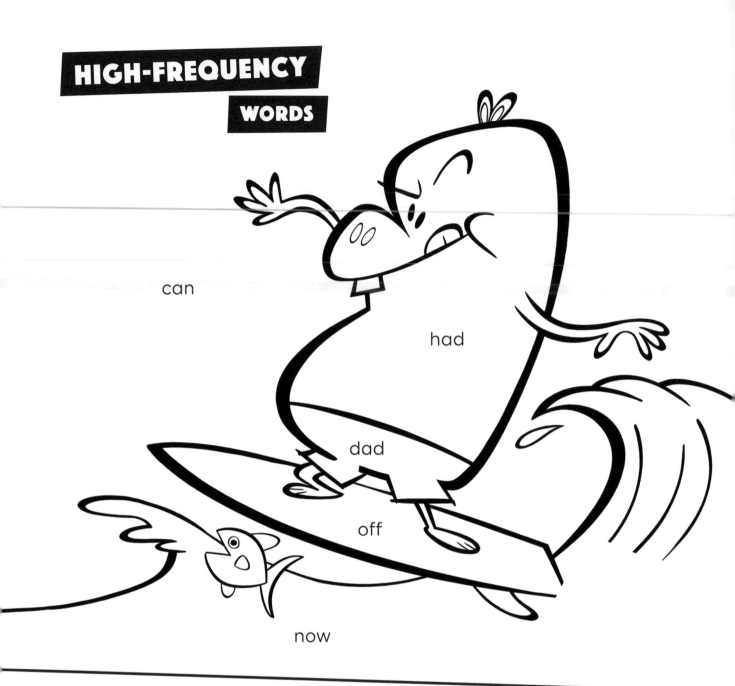

can

had

dad

off

now

Use the paint-by-words chart to complete the picture. Use crayons, pencils, or paint!

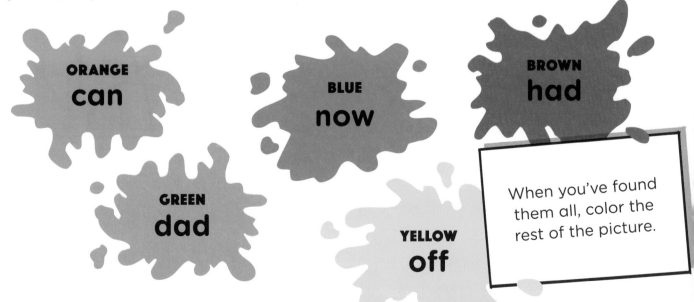

ORANGE
can

BLUE
now

BROWN
had

GREEN
dad

YELLOW
off

When you've found them all, color the rest of the picture.

Trace the dotted letters.

off

can

dad

had

now

HIGH-FREQUENCY WORDS

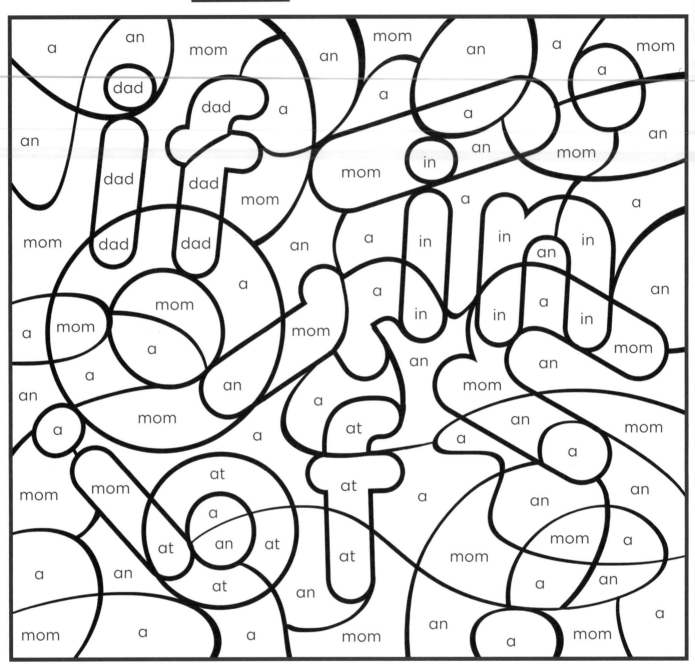

Use the paint-by-words chart to complete the picture and find the hidden words. Use crayons, pencils, or paint!

PURPLE
to

YELLOW
but

RED
mom

ORANGE
I

BROWN
got

BLUE
no

Trace the dotted letters.

MATH CONCEPTS & VOCABULARY

COUNTING SHEEP

Help Shang High fall asleep by counting the sheep. Choose the correct number to write in the spaces.

- - - - - - - - - - - - - - - -   - - - - - - - - - - - - - - - -

- - - - - - - - - - - - - - - -   - - - - - - - - - - - - - - - -

- - - - - - - - - - - - - - - -   - - - - - - - - - - - - - - - -

COUNT WITH SHANG HIGH

Shang High is planning his birthday party! Count the items and choose the correct number to write in each space.

CHOOSE HERE

1   2   3   4   5   6   7   8   9   10

1.

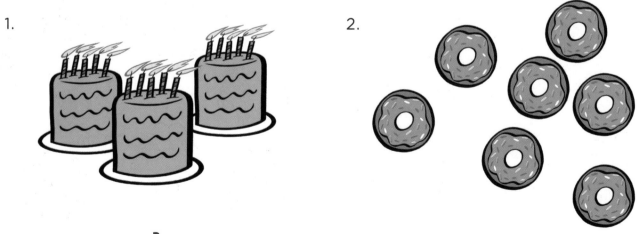

3

2.

3.

4.

5.

6.

7.

8.

Count the number of cookies in these groups. Choose the correct number to write in each space.

CHOOSE HERE

1   2   3   4   5   6   7   8   9   10

1.

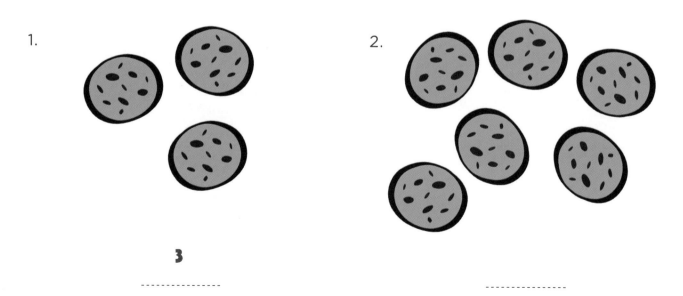

3

2.

3.

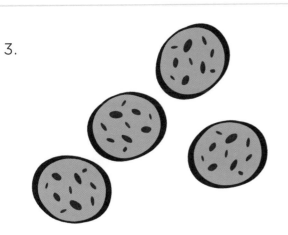

4.

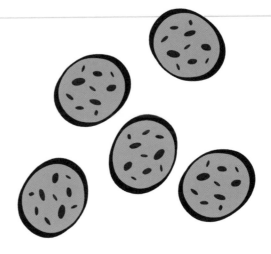

5.

6.

7.

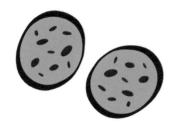

8.

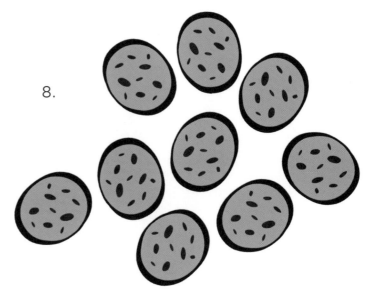

Count the number of animals in each group.

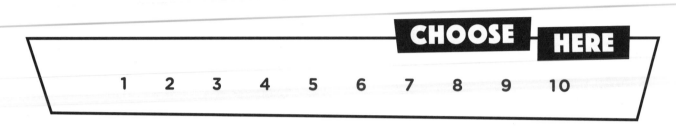

CHOOSE HERE

1 2 3 4 5 6 7 8 9 10

1. There are _____ bees in this swarm.

2. There are _____ cows in this herd.

3. There are _____ sheep in this flock.

4. There are _____ fish in this school.

5. There are _____ ants in this colony.

6. There are _____ wolves in this pack.

WHICH HAS MORE?

Circle the group that has more.

1.

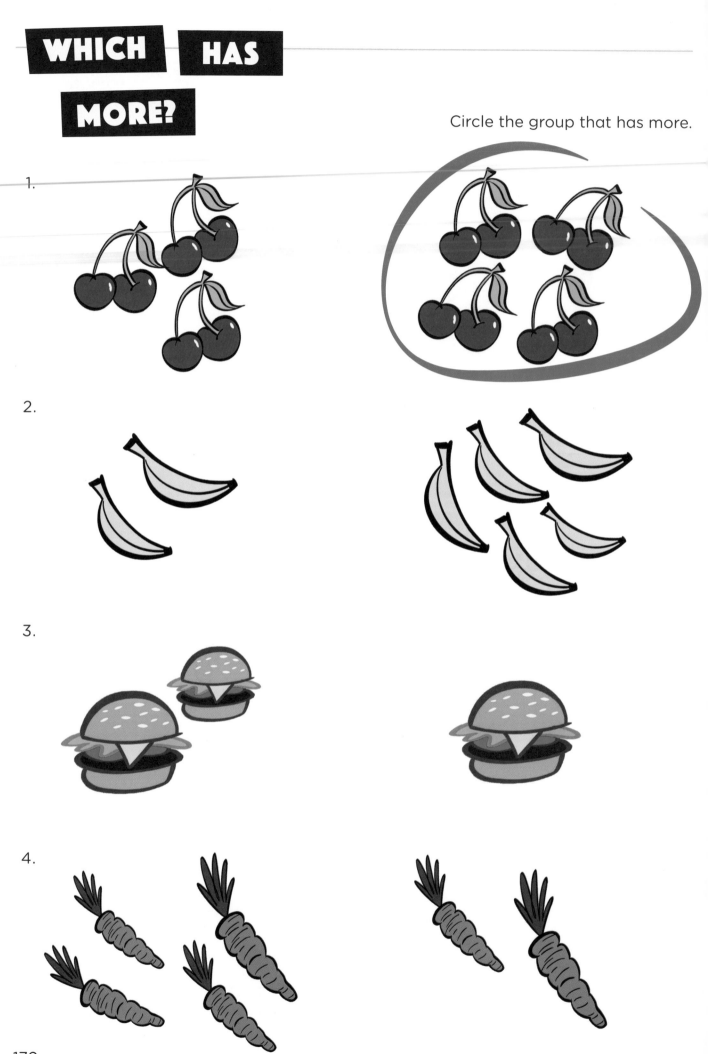

2.

3.

4.

Circle the group that has fewer.

1.

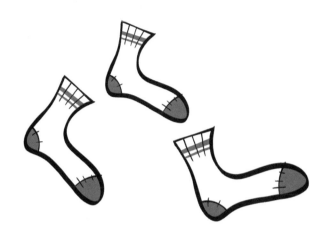

2.

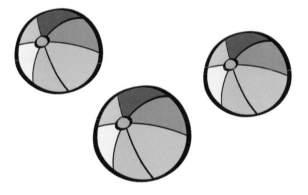

3.

4.

Circle which is bigger.

Circle which is smaller.

Circle who is shorter.

Circle which is taller.

Circle which is lighter.

Circle who is heavier.

PATTERNS

Continue the pattern by coloring in the white circles.

1.

2.

3.

4.

5.

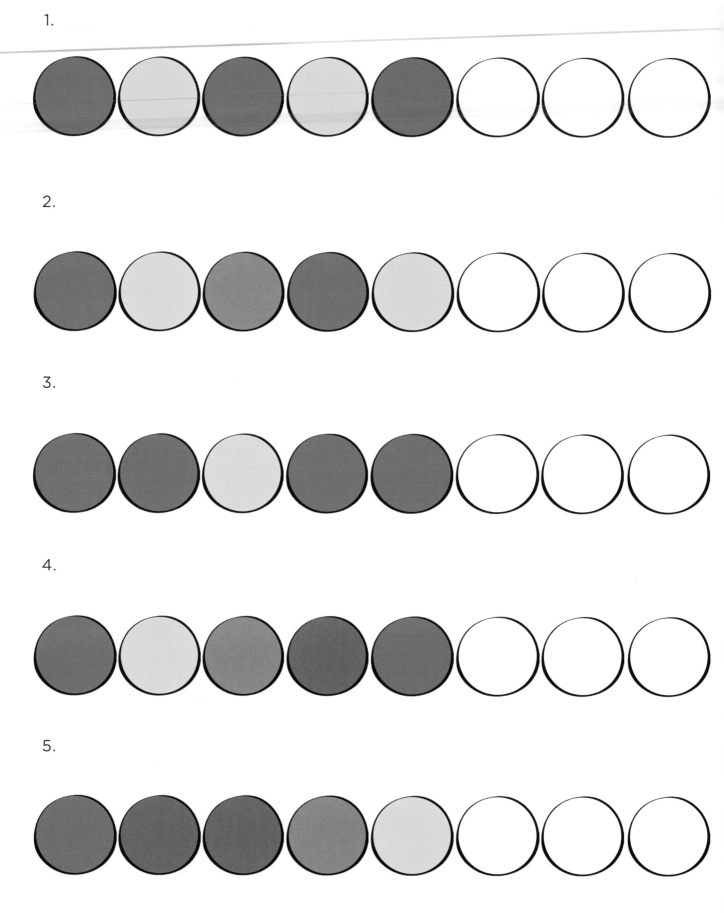

Fill in the missing pattern by coloring in the white circles.

1.

2.

3.

4.

5.

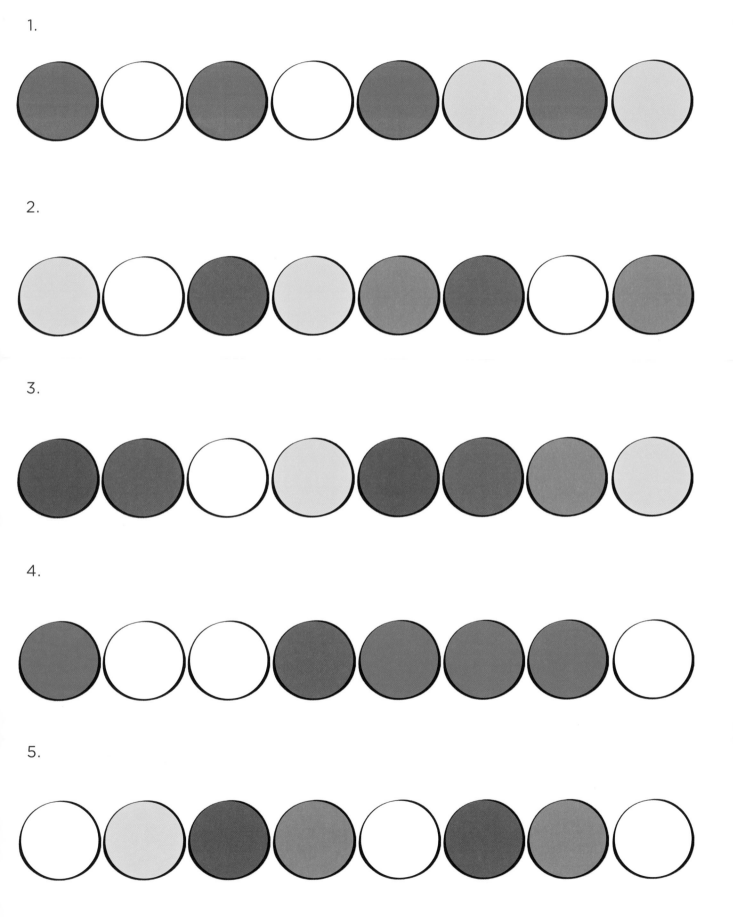

NUMBER BONDS

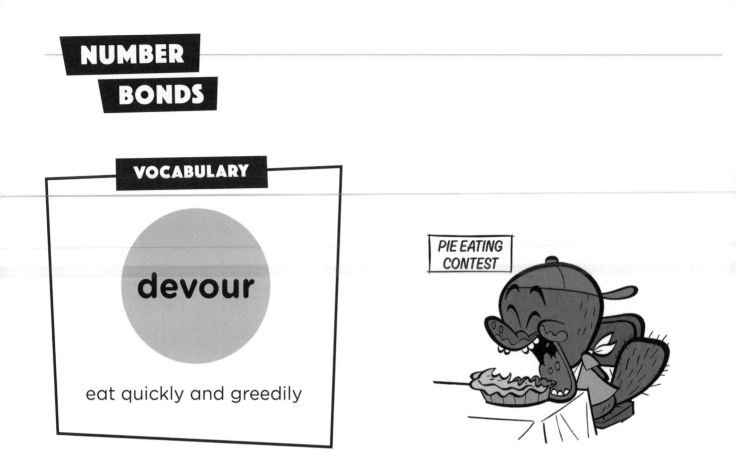

VOCABULARY

devour

eat quickly and greedily

PIE EATING CONTEST

Use the stack of pies (or your fingers) to help you complete the number bonds.

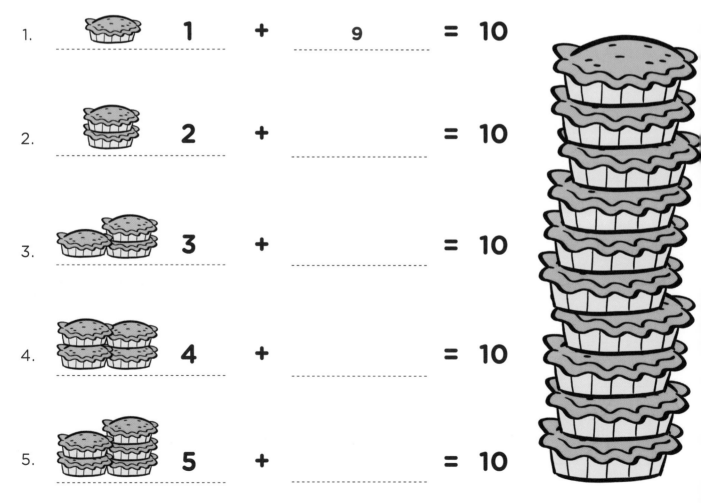

1. $1 + 9 = 10$

2. $2 + = 10$

3. $3 + = 10$

4. $4 + = 10$

5. $5 + = 10$

2D SHAPES

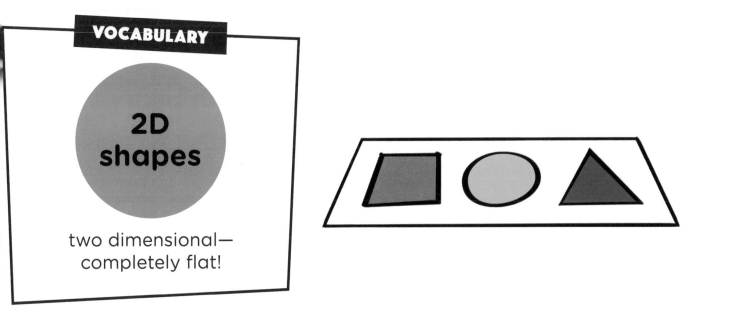

VOCABULARY

2D shapes

two dimensional—completely flat!

Draw a line with your pencil and match each shape to its name.

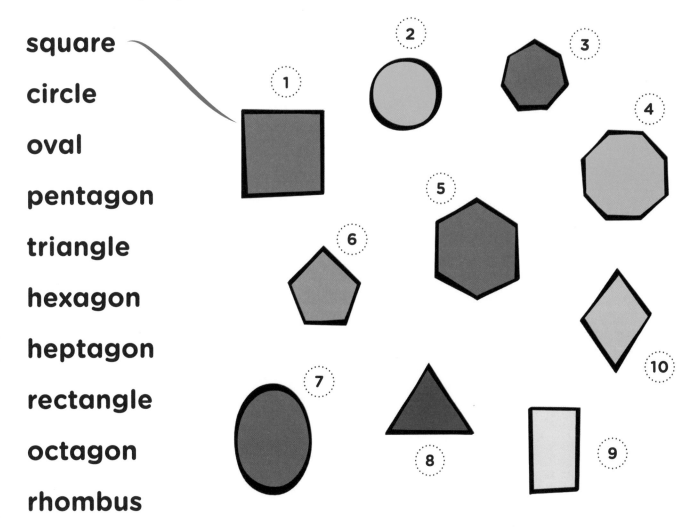

square

circle

oval

pentagon

triangle

hexagon

heptagon

rectangle

octagon

rhombus

LISTENING, SPEAKING, CREATING

Shang High is listening with his whole body.

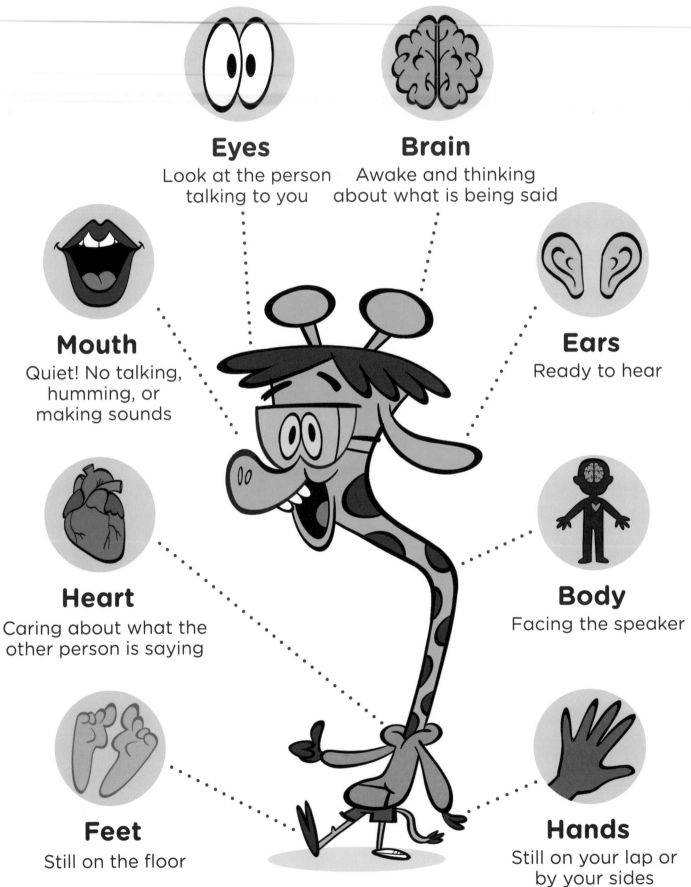

Eyes
Look at the person talking to you

Brain
Awake and thinking about what is being said

Mouth
Quiet! No talking, humming, or making sounds

Ears
Ready to hear

Heart
Caring about what the other person is saying

Body
Facing the speaker

Feet
Still on the floor

Hands
Still on your lap or by your sides

THIS IS MY FAMILY

HI! MY NAME IS

_____

Draw your me-moji:

I AM

_____

YEARS OLD

Circle a me-moji that shows how you feel.

MY FRIENDS ARE:

_____

_____

_____

_____

HAPPY

CONFUSED

SAD

SILLY

MISCHIEVOUS

Teddy Talks are about creating something new and sharing it with the world!

grips

handlebar

brake

grip tape

fork

deck

wheel

VOCABULARY

scooter

a vehicle with two wheels

Design your own scooter on the next page.
Use some of ours for inspiration!

Scooter of the future

DESIGN ON NEXT PAGE

Design your own scooter here.

TEDDY Talks **DESIGN** **YOUR** **OWN** **DRONE**

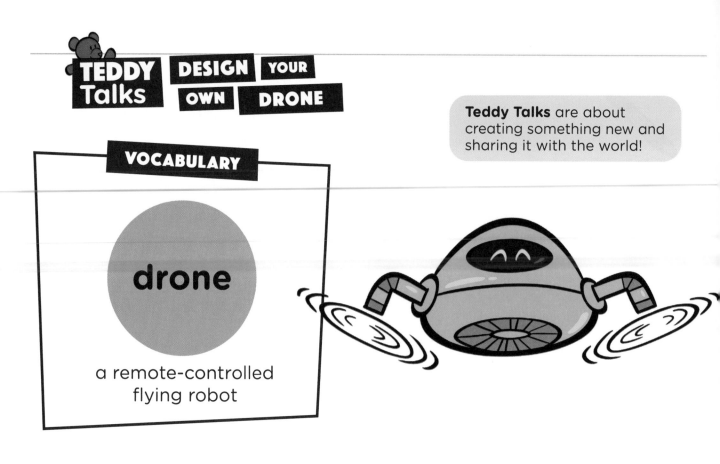

VOCABULARY

drone

a remote-controlled flying robot

Design your own drone on the next page.
Don't forget to give it a name!
These are parts used to make a drone.

propeller

battery

camera

controller

motor

DESIGN ON NEXT PAGE

Design your own drone here.

PAGE 38-39

A	B	C	D	E	F
G	H	I	J	K	L
M	N	O	P	Q	R
S	T	U	V	W	X
Y	Z				

PAGE 43

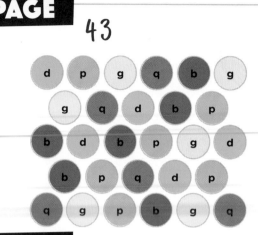

PAGE 118

Your answers might include:

cab, dab, jab, lab,
bat, cat, hat, sat,
bad, dad, mad, sad,
ban, man, pan, van,
bag, hag, nag, rag,
cap, gap, map, rap,
bam, ham, jam, yam,
gal, pal, yak, wax

PAGE 119

Your answers might include:

bed, fed, red, led,
beg, leg, peg,
bet, get, jet, pet,
den, hen, men, pen

PAGE 120

Your answers might include:

bit, fit, kit, sit,
bid, did, kid, lid,
big, dig, gig, wig,
dim, him, rim,
dip, hip, lip, zip,
bin, pin, sin, tin

PAGE 121

Your answers might include:

cot, dot, hot, pot,
cob, job, mob, sob,
cog, dog, hog, jog,
cop, hop, mop, top,
box, fox, mom

PAGE 122

Your answers might include:

but, cut, gut, nut,
cub, rud, sub, tub,
bug, dug, jug, rug,
bum, gum, sum,
bun, fun, nun, sun,
bud, dud, mud,
pup, cup, bus

PAGE 123

1. **kiss**   4. **duck**

2. **bell**   5. **mess**

3. **buzz**   6. **dress**

PAGE 124-125

1. cat
2. jump
3. hand
4. back
5. wish
6. red
7. box
8. fish
9. egg
10. bus

PAGE 128-129

Nonreal words:

3. hig
4. fim
5. mub
10. mab
12. mup
18. dat
19. mit

PAGE 132-133

Nonreal words:

4. kezz
11. juck
12. zoth
13. coss
14. shup
16. rell

PAGE 136

small

PAGE 137

sad

PAGE 138-139

1. on
2. in
3. beneath
4. behind
5. in front of
6. next to

PAGE 146

PAGE 147

PAGE 148

PAGE 149

PAGE 150

PAGE 151

1. **happy**

2. **crying**

3. **angry**

4. **laughing**

5. **sad**

PAGE 162–163

1. **1 sheep**

2. **2 sheep**

3. **3 sheep**

4. **4 sheep**

5. **5 sheep**

6. **6 sheep**

7. **7 sheep**

8. **8 sheep**

9. **9 sheep**

10. **10 sheep**

PAGE 164–165

1. **3 cakes**

2. **7 donuts**

3. **4 balloons**

4. **9 candles**

5. **5 party hats**

6. **6 presents**

7. **2 pizzas**

8. **1 piñata**

PAGE 166–167

1. **3 cookies**

2. **6 cookies**

3. **4 cookies**

4. **5 cookies**

5. **8 cookies**

6. **7 cookies**

7. **2 cookies**

8. **9 cookies**

PAGE 168–169

1. **10 bees**

2. **5 cows**

3. **3 sheep**

4. **4 fish**

5. **9 ants**

6. **6 wolves**

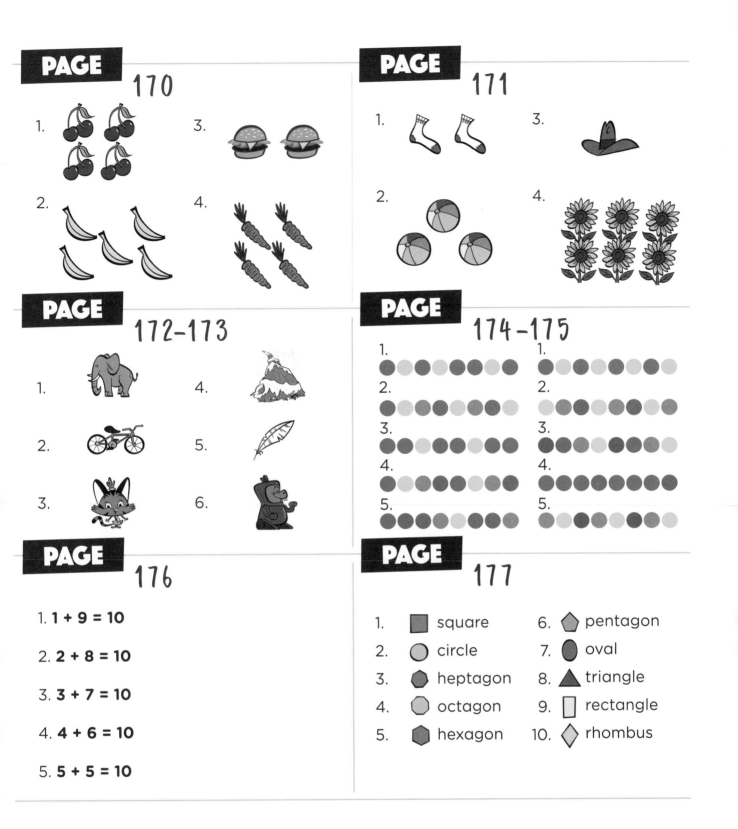

PAGE 170

1. [cherries]
2. [bananas]
3. [hamburgers]
4. [carrots]

PAGE 171

1. [socks]
2. [beach balls]
3. [hat]
4. [sunflowers]

PAGE 172–173

1. [elephant]
2. [bicycle]
3. [cat]
4. [mountain]
5. [feather]
6. [gorilla]

PAGE 174–175

1. [dots]
2. [dots]
3. [dots]
4. [dots]
5. [dots]

1. [dots]
2. [dots]
3. [dots]
4. [dots]
5. [dots]

PAGE 176

1. **1 + 9 = 10**

2. **2 + 8 = 10**

3. **3 + 7 = 10**

4. **4 + 6 = 10**

5. **5 + 5 = 10**

PAGE 177

1. ■ square
2. ● circle
3. ⬣ heptagon
4. ⬡ octagon
5. ⬢ hexagon
6. ⬠ pentagon
7. ⬭ oval
8. ▲ triangle
9. ▭ rectangle
10. ◇ rhombus

189

MEET THE
MRS WORDSMITH TEAM

Editor-in-Chief
Sofia Fenichell

Associate Creative Director
Lady San Pedro

Art Director
Craig Kellman

Writers

Tatiana Barnes

Mark Holland
Sawyer Eaton

Amelia Mehra

Researcher
Eleni Savva

Lexicographer
Ian Brookes

Designers

Suzanne Bullat
James Sales

Fabrice Gourdel
James Webb
Holly Jones

Caroline Henriksen
Jess Macadam

Producers
Eva Schumacher Payne
Leon Welters

Academic Advisors
Emma Madden
Prof. Susan Neuman

Project Managers
Senior Editor Helen Murray
Design Manager Sunita Gahir

Senior Production Editor Jennifer Murray
Senior Production Controller Louise Minihane
Publishing Director Mark Searle

DK Delhi
DTP Designers Satish Gaur and Rohit Rojal
Senior DTP Designer Pushpak Tyagi
Pre-production Manager Sunil Sharma
Managing Art Editor Romi Chakraborty

DK would like to thank Anna Formanek for design assistance,
and Roohi Sehgal, Lisa Stock, and Julia March for
editorial assistance.

First American Edition, 2022
Published in the United States by DK Publishing
1745 Broadway, 20th Floor, New York NY 10019

Variations of this content are available as
printable worksheets at mrswordsmith.com

24 25 26 10 9 8 7 6 5 4 3
005–325946–Jan/2022

A catalog record for this book
is available from the Library of Congress.
ISBN 978-0-7440-5152-0

Printed and bound in Malaysia

www.dk.com

mrswordsmith.com

For the curious

This book was made with
Forest Stewardship Council™
certified paper—one small
step in DK's commitment to
a sustainable future.

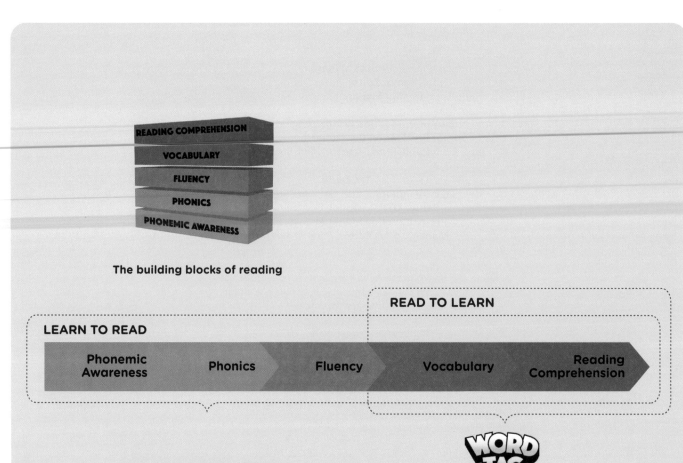

The building blocks of reading

READ TO LEARN

LEARN TO READ

| Phonemic Awareness | Phonics | Fluency | Vocabulary | Reading Comprehension |

Readiculous App
App Store & Google Play

Word Tag App
App Store & Google Play

OUR JOB IS TO INCREASE YOUR CHILD'S READING AGE

This book adheres to the science of reading. Our research-backed learning helps children progress through phonemic awareness, phonics, fluency, vocabulary, and reading comprehension.